Contents

Autism: debates and testimonies

by

DENYS RIBAS

Translated by Sophie Leighton

First published by
© Presses Universitaires de France (Le Fil Rouge) as
Controverses sur l'autisme et témoignages
Paris, 2004

Denys Ribas, 2004

Published in the United Kingdom

by Free Association Books
London, 2006

British Library Cataloguing in Publication Data
A catalogue record for this book is available from the British Library

Produced by Bookchase, London
Printed and bound in the EU by Bell & Bain Ltd., Glasgow

ISBN 1853439088

Preface

THE PUBLICATION OF this book in the English language pays tribute to the many English texts on which it has drawn. A genuine debate strikes me as particularly necessary now that it is in serious prospect, with a growing interest in dialogue emerging from a range of professionals in this field. This is certainly the case in the United Kingdom, to judge by the publication of *Autism and Personality: Findings from the Tavistock Autism Workshop*, edited by Anne Alvarez and Susan Reid,[1] which appeared in French translation after I had written my book. While presenting a strong case for respecting the clinical individuality of each child, this work demonstrated a keen interest both in cognitive research, with a re-examination of the concept of a defence that leads to a disorganisation through the traumatic effect of the overwhelming excitation, and in an investigation of trauma and a consideration of the body, which reveal points of convergence with the views that I have been advocating.

I hope to contribute to stimulating this scientific debate, from which patients and families stand to be the foremost beneficiaries.

Denys Ribas

---

[1] London, Routledge, 1999.

Introduction

AUTISM IS A subject that generates debate and passion – partly because of the nature of this pathology, which is simultaneously strange, alarming, fascinating and inaccessible, and partly because of the challenge it represents to our understanding of the origins of human communication and language in particular, as the source of that which defines human nature. The lack of consensus is frankly bewildering for parents, and the obstacles to any dispassionate consideration of the hypotheses constitute a major impediment to progress in the understanding and treatment of childhood autism.

However, in the last decade, the debate has been enriched by cognitive research, which has led to controversy between various standpoints, shedding light on clinical practice from different perspectives. At the same time, the publication of testimonies from former autistic patients is providing a revealing inside perspective on autism, with all the impact that first-hand experience can have. In order to open up a serious debate here between cognitive and psychoanalytic theories, as I am aware that my clinical account necessarily draws on my own convictions, I shall mainly be quoting directly from the patients themselves, who have found the remarkable courage to share their experiences with us. These comparisons that set out the disagreements also reveal some striking points of convergence. Revisiting the work of Hans Asperger, the precursor of the institutional treatment of autism, which he described during the same period as Leo Kanner, it becomes clear how artificial some of the recent divergences are. New questions also arise from the assisted written productions of some autistic people, as well as from developments in genetics.[1]

Kanner's original description in 1942 in the United States refers to an affective disorder of communication through eleven clinical cases that demonstrate the inability to communicate (even when the child has some language) and the autistic child's need for *aloneness* and for *sameness*, observing that this is an innate disorder. At the outset, however, as a psychiatrist Kanner was struck by the specific attitude of certain parents, which was cold and distant. This viewpoint has no connection with psychoanalysis: Kanner was not a psychoanalyst and it was he who first posed a paradox that would fuel several decades of debate: how is an

[1] In this book, I have drawn on texts and cases studied in the monthly research seminar on autism at the children's day hospital at *Entraide Universitaire,* and I would like to thank its participants.

innate disorder – which implies an aetiology that precedes birth and early relationships – connected with a relational difficulty on the part of parents, which would only have an influence after the child's birth?

Margaret Mahler, the psychoanalyst, then provided an account of autism as the failure of a healthy and normal symbiosis between mother and child at birth, in which the child resorts to a negative hallucination of the external world, which she contrasts with the alternative pathological outcome – symbiotic psychosis – in which the child hallucinates an omnipotent and terrifying mother with whom fusion is artificially preserved.

Bettelheim's therapeutic standpoint that the child should be separated from his parents was then crudely equated with the psychoanalytic view of autism because of the impact that his work had in the United States and then in France with the films of Tony Lainé and Daniel Karlin. However, it should be pointed out that Bettelheim's theoretical standpoint is much more subtle than this. His view is in fact that the child becomes autistic and his parents fail to cure him of this through their inability to tolerate their rejection *by* the child. It is nevertheless true that Bettelheim's countertransference towards parents is not very positive. Thus, on the next page in *Truants from Life*,[2] he describes how some parents ruined their child's life with an extremely rigid upbringing and by leaving him to sleep, without responding to his cries, in a room with an open window on a freezing cold night: in the morning, the child's urine had frozen around him and he had to spend many months in hospital, during which his mental health suffered because he then developed a psychosis. However, this terrifying example of a deficient parental attitude has nothing to do with autism! It probably emerges into the text after his theoretical reflections concerning the parents' innocence in order to annul this, in an inadvertent expression of the author's underlying attitudes. Frances Tustin, who conducted brilliant investigations into the treatment of autism, refers to Bettelheim's views on parents as 'both cruel and erroneous' (1986, p. 65).[3]

Bettelheim's deeply held belief in the responsibility of the environment and in its therapeutic potential does not in fact stem from his analytic experience – analysts are wary of adopting reparative standpoints towards the patient – but from his tragic experience in the concentration camp. It was there that he was able to observe how an intensely hostile environment could drive a human being to the depths of despair and totally destroy

---

2 Bettelheim, B. *Truants from Life: The Rehabilitation of Emotionally Disturbed Children*. Glencoe, IL: Free Press, 1955.

3 Tustin, F. *Autistic Barriers in Neurotic Patients*. London, Karnac, 1986.

his hope in the outside world. Some deportees withdrew into themselves, even right into the ground – which is why their fellow deportees called them 'the Muslims' by analogy with the prayer position – and very soon died. Bettelheim was profoundly struck by the similarity between the autistic retreat and the retreat of the 'Muslim' deportee. It was this that inspired him with the powerful concept that something that could be created by a hostile environment could be healed by a restorative one. This idea has continuing relevance. The case of the children who were discovered in Romanian orphanages, presenting stereotypies (autistic symptoms) and brain lesions such as cortical atrophies caused by relational deprivation, lends support to this view: once they were moved into a warm and stimulating environment, these orphans developed rapidly, showing a favourable regression in their brain anomalies.

In its application to autism, however, this model of deprivation and the therapeutic decision to separate the child from his parents openly led to the attribution of responsibility for the child's illness to the parents and encountered – alas – their own sense of guilt. Gradually, therefore, a rebellion stirred against Bettelheim's views among some professionals and among parents.

However, it would be unfortunate to reduce Bettelheim's entire body of work to his viewpoint on parents or to tyrannical attitudes that he may have had in his institution in order to dismiss it out of hand. When an autistic child opens up to the world and goes back through stages that normal children experience at a much earlier age, caregivers and parents are required to respond at early relational levels and they would be mad not to do so: the problematic of a new psychic birth is not easy to overcome, however straightforward it may appear. It is difficult to know whether to accompany the child at this level of regression – at the risk of denying his chronological age – or to maintain higher expectations of him at the risk of breaking up a developmental process that has resumed its course. A particularly good example of this is the persistence of toilet-training difficulties in a child who is beginning to discover language: is it better to impose toilet-training on him (or at least attempt it) in order to launch him on the path to socialisation or to allow an opportunity for a normal integration of sphincter control and for the emergence of language to take place?

The criticism generally made of psychoanalysts by parents' associations who impute Bettelheimian views to them is therefore correct in one sense and in another sense completely wrong.

It should be conceded that in the 1950s psychoanalysis had a naïve belief in the creative force of psychic life in the environment, and this naïvety – not very psychoanalytic! – warrants criticism. This also applies to Winnicott and his *aetiological* views on autism. However, French psychoanalysts did not hold the same therapeutic standpoints as Bettelheim. The creation of *day* hospitals was manifestly based on the premise that it was beneficial for the child to remain in his family and for the family to be included in the therapeutic process!

With the reaction against Bettelheim by Eric Schopler, a former colleague of his, in the United States, as part of an entirely understandable oppositional trend, the debate became obscured to the point of impossibility for many years.

Schopler postulated that autism was caused by an organic 'handicap' and he therefore thought that there were no psychic defences at work in the child but a permanent incapacity. He considered the child as a handicapped person who needed to be re-educated with the aid of parents, who were permitted to work alongside therapists. Paradoxically, this viewpoint, which ultimately denied any hope to parents, thereby protecting them from the grim wait for the miracle that never came, brought immense relief to parents (with good reason since they were told what to do and their dignity was restored to them). However, despite its humanistic claims (provided that it is non-violent) based on behavioural techniques and its felicitously analgesic quality for parents, I have strongly criticised this method[4] on the grounds that it abandons any therapeutic ambition, denies the child's suffering and reinforces his failure to emerge as an individual subject.

Furthermore, a confusion between cause and effect about which I have long wondered has persistently skewed the debate. In fact, a handicap is the result of an illness or an accident – whatever the cause – rather than the cause itself. The premise of an organic origin has been regarded as a certainty and it has been taken for granted that this excluded any possibility of a relational therapy proving effective. This method has also monopolised education as a banner, as its acronym – the TEACCH method – makes explicit, whereas in fact it is behaviourism supplemented with modern educational theory (Seguin, Freinet and Montessori). Confusion has thus been fostered between therapy and educational theory, as between education and schooling. This is why some parents today are demanding for their child to be integrated in school, as the only form of treatment,

[4] Ribas, D. *Un cri obscur, l'énigme des enfants autistes* [A muted cry: the enigma of autistic children]. Paris, Calmann-Lévy, 1992.

when in fact it is impossible to see why an autistic child with these capacities would not benefit from both psychic treatment and schooling.

A possible source of this misunderstanding lies in the particularly stringent conditions applied to treatment by medical insurance companies in the United States. Funding for treatment had not been established, whereas schooling was guaranteed to every American citizen, and Schopler was able to obtain federal funds for teaching 'handicapped' children. Across the Atlantic, this utilitarian ideology worked in reverse: France spends more on caring for its sick than enabling handicapped people to lead worthwhile lives, which may be understandable in terms of traumatological efficacy, but this distinction is certainly entirely inadequate in child psychiatry. Militant parents therefore rejected psychiatry on the basis of several misunderstandings, even if they reduced the funding made available for treating their children in the process. In fact, they wanted other forms of treatment than those being offered by French psychiatrists at the time.

The dispute reached its height of absurdity when a private bill of law was tabled for the recognition of autism as originating from a handicap, whereas in scientific terms it is a severely disabling illness of unknown origin. It would have been more appropriate to ask the courts to decide how society should care for the handicaps resulting from autism. During her time in office, Simone Veil had in fact acknowledged the need to remove the barrier between caring for autistic people and treating their handicap: they required the combined resources of the health service and community health. Regrettably, the economic crisis of the 1990s restricted the scope of this advance.

CHAPTER 1

Hans Asperger's neglected account of autism

I HAVE CHOSEN to pay tribute to Asperger's long neglected text in order to restore it to life for readers who are unfamiliar with this clinical account of autism. In fact, Asperger's work bears some striking similarities with Kanner's research[1] and he seems to deserve as much credit as Kanner for discovering this syndrome. Since Asperger's work was brought back into favour by Loma Wing in 1981 in the United Kingdom, his contribution has generally been restricted to his description of autistic components in the personalities of highly intellectual individuals – grouped under the name of the syndrome to which he gave his name in the international classification.

ICD-10 gives the following definition of Asperger's syndrome: 'A disorder of uncertain nosological validity, characterized by the same kind of qualitative abnormalities of reciprocal social interaction that typify autism, together with a restricted, stereotyped, repetitive repertoire of interests and activities. The disorder differs from autism primarily in that there is no general delay or retardation in language or in cognitive development. Most individuals are of normal general intelligence but it is common for them to be markedly clumsy ... There is a strong tendency for the abnormalities to persist into adolescence and adult life ... Psychotic episodes occasionally occur in early adult life'.[2]

However, a careful reading of Asperger's text 'Die 'autistischen Psychopathen' im Kindesalter' ['Autistic psychopaths' in childhood']'[3] uncovers a general portrait of childhood autism.

This text is Asperger's doctoral thesis, which he defended in 1943 and published in 1944. As we know, Kanner's text dates from 1942. However, whereas Kanner describes children he has seen in consultation, Asperger describes children for whom he has been caring since 1926 in a therapeutic institution at which he became a clinical consultant in 1930. We will also see how far in this context, which was isolated from

---

1 Described in my 1992 book, *Un cri obscur, l'énigme des enfants autistes* [A muted cry: the enigma of autistic children]. Paris, Calmann-Lévy.

2 *ICD-10 Classification of Mental and Behavioural Disorders: Clinical Descriptions and Diagnostic Guidelines*. Geneva: World Health Organization, 1992, p. 258.

3 *Archiv für Psychiatrie und Nervenkrankheiten*, Berlin, 1944, 117: 76–136 – page references are to this edition, for quotations translated here.

developments in the United States by the war, Asperger's extremely outdated organic aetiological presuppositions led to the establishment of a treatment that privileged the affective relationship. This had a very different influence on the ideological perspectives generated by childhood autism from those in recent years, in a way that is highly instructive to consider.

Hans Asperger was born in Vienna in 1906 and died there in 1980. When he mentioned in the course of a lecture that he enjoyed scouting and mountain excursions, some concerns arose as to whether he might have participated in the Hitler youth movement and subscribed to Nazi ideology. This was not the case, according to Jacques Constant, author of the preface to the French edition of his book,[4] who also points out that treating children with abnormalities in the 1930s was itself antithetical to Nazism. In fact, one of the reasons that Asperger first became interested in autism was that, having always enjoyed taking his young patients to the summer camps in the mountains, he discovered there that autistic children reacted in terror instead of taking advantage of the opportunity to share his love of nature.

Although his tutor, Erwin Lazar, had been interested in Freud's ideas and had invited some psychoanalysts to work in his clinic, he subsequently took the view that psychoanalysis was not appropriate for childhood disorders. Asperger subscribed to his tutor's ideas, taking a standpoint that Constant describes as '*apsychoanalytic*'. Lazar had undertaken to treat children and adolescents who had particularly suffered during the First World War. This interest in children traumatised by war may have contributed to bringing more humanity into medical tradition. Lazar's successor later responded in turn to the same need after the Second World War.

Asperger then developed a therapeutic educational methodology – the term *Heilpädagogik* was introduced in Vienna in 1911 by Clemens von Pirquet – as a practice of institutional treatment that gradually infused the exclusively paediatric hospital tradition from which it emerged with a remarkable humanism (as Uta Frith emphasises). Asperger described his theory of therapeutic education as a specific approach that should not be confused with re-education, an intuitive synthesis of medical and educational practice and a tool of reference intended for doctors and nurses and for teachers and therapists alike. As we will see, for this author, knowledge of any child requires a lively affective relationship with him.

---

[4] *Les psychopathes autistiques pendant l'enfance*, translated by E. Wagner, N. Rivollier and D. L'Hôpital, Le Plessis-Robinson, Institut Synthélabo pour le progrès de la connaissance, 1998.

Asperger's aetiological theories: constitution and heredity

Although Asperger initially asserts that the individual defies classification, his theory of mental disorders is rooted in a particularly outmoded tradition based on pathological constitution and hereditary degeneracy. He refers here to Kretschmer, for whom 'the bodily and the psychic constitutions correspond down to the finest details' (p. 77). Kretschmer tended to attribute manic-depressive states to patients who belonged to the 'pyknic' physical type – short and corpulent – and schizophrenia to tall, thin, 'leptosome' patients. Asperger returns to the question of typology in the conclusion of his text, in particular associating autistic psychopaths with Jung's 'introverted thinking' type, but he observes that this discussion is not strictly productive because the clinical profiles outlined in the literature have not been described in relation to childhood behaviour.

For Asperger, there is no doubt that autism is hereditary. He states that the fathers usually work in intellectual professions and are ill at ease when this is not the case. The 'quirks and peculiarities' of well-known artists and scholars are often perpetuated in their descendants, whereas their greatness is lost. Asperger shows his adherence to theories of degeneracy here. 'These discoveries about heredity therefore support the hereditary basis for the characteristics of this condition, as well as the powerful legacy of the disposition', he concludes (p. 129). Observing that several of his cases are only children, he denies that living only with adults contributes to the child's autism. 'These children's autism does not arise from the unfavourable influences to which an only child is exposed in his upbringing, but it originates from the dispositions that he inherits from parents who are also autistic' (p. 130). Accordingly, he goes on to describe characterological abnormalities in the parents, and is surprised to find that one mother has the qualities of an abstract intelligence that he nevertheless considers to be self-evidently intrinsically masculine, whereas women are predisposed towards concrete realities! 'The autistic psychopath is an extreme variant of masculine intelligence and character' (p. 129). In his preface, Jacques Constant points out how these theories were then adopted by the sexist ideology of the time: 'This is not far removed from the three Ks – *Küche*, *Kirche*, *Kinder*. The mood of the day that relegated women to "kitchen, church and children" can thus perhaps be discerned here in Asperger's text'.

The other aetiology of autism that he considers is also organic, relating to pathologies in pregnancy and labour.

An interest in the child's whole personality and his individuality

In contrast, however, when he is assessing his young patients, Asperger takes a highly contemporary stand against the danger of reification under the pretext of objectivisation. 'We believe that a person's nature only reveals itself accurately and faithfully to someone capable of perceiving it when he lives with this person and can observe the numerous reactions that occur for him in everyday life, in his work, study and play, both when demands are made on him and during spontaneous activity in a free and relaxed situation. Every artificially constructed situation, including any test conditions, carries the risk that the child will present himself in a different way from usual, being somewhat inhibited and hampered by fear. He may overcompensate for his insecurity and sensitivity to contact with extreme behaviour, or alternatively exhort himself to special achievements of which he is not ordinarily capable at school or in community life' (p. 82).

Asperger then explains that in order to know the child's 'essential character traits and emotional nature', some educational responsibilities and some strictness towards him are required for establishing a relationship. These characteristics only reveal themselves 'to the person who belongs to this lively unity that exists between the guide and the child, this unity of reacting to each other in numerous conscious and yet more unconscious exchanges. The child under observation will only disclose his deepest nature to the person who stands alongside him in a learning situation' (pp. 82–83).

Asperger's patients

Fritz V...

Following a normal birth, Fritz spoke his first words at the early age of ten months, and was soon talking in an adult way. However, he could not walk until he was fourteen months old and he was dependent and clumsy for a long time. Asperger describes him as follows: 'From a very early age, he behaved in a way that made his upbringing extremely difficult; he refused to obey any orders, simply doing whatever he wanted or the exact opposite of what he was told. He has always been very restless and unstable; he can leave nothing alone and has to pick everything up, investigating everything and ignoring any restrictive prohibitions. He has a pronounced destructive drive and he soon tears and breaks anything he gets his hands on' (p. 86).

Fritz was incapable of playing with other children, and would sometimes hit them very wildly without any thought for the consequences. When he took a hammer to his fellow pupils, he was thrown out of the nursery school on his first day! (He had also demolished the coat-hangers.) Lacking any affective relationship, he might hug anyone, but it was like an attack. He seemed unable to love anyone and to be insensitive to criticism and impervious to blame. Instead, he seemed to like annoying the teacher with his mischievous behaviour and his negativity.

His mother, who resembles him, came from a family of 'slightly mad geniuses', some of whom had been famous. When she arrived at the clinic with her son, Asperger was struck by the way in which she walked 'without looking around her, arms folded behind her back, with the boy beside her doing whatever he liked, running up and down – it looked as if they had nothing to do with each other' (p. 87). He adds that this woman from a high social class was unkempt and dirty herself and unable to take physical care of her child. When she could no longer tolerate the household situation, she had gone away and left her husband and two sons in order to spend a week or so in the mountains that she liked.

Physically, Fritz was a tall and fine-looking boy, with an 'aristocratic' face that was no longer childlike. 'He has a strange gaze: generally, when it does not have a plainly malicious glint, it is directed into empty space, without looking properly at the person facing him, which is what forms the foundation of conversational contact; he seems only to glance across people and things with fleeting "peripheral" looks. It is as if he were "not really there" ' (p. 87). He spoke in a particular way, rarely replying spontaneously to questions, sometimes repeating a single word or singing, 'I don't like to say that, I don't like to say that' (p. 88). Talking very slowly, in a high-pitched, monotonous voice with no speech melody, he would also modify certain words by lengthening them and modulating their pitch, which gave his language a melopoeic quality.

In the treatment institution, Fritz displayed great difficulties relating to other people and he was unable to live in a community. He kept himself apart and seemed indifferent to those around him, but would respond to direct or indirect requests with aggressive or destructive behaviour. He also often reacted with stereotypies, which appeared for no external reason: batting his eyelids when spoken to, making sweeping gestures to strike his legs, or jumping around in the room. Asperger noted that this reaction seemed to stem from an experience of 'unwanted intrusion into his closeted personality' (p. 88).

Fritz had other strange forms of behaviour: he would eat entire pencils and large quantities of paper. He would also lick the table and spread his saliva everywhere.

Fritz's 'maliciousness'

With this word, which is unusual nowadays in a scientific context but which aptly indicates the demands made on other people's emotional responses, Asperger describes remarkably well how the child attacks those around him and the theoretical problems that this causes: how can a child who is indifferent to the world have such an aptitude for provoking violent reactions? It is because they appear to have such an unerring sense of what is most unpleasant, painful and dangerous in any given situation that 'these children's malicious behaviour appears to be so "sophisticated" ' (p. 88). 'This boy, who just lolled in his chair with a vacant expression, would suddenly jump up, eyes gleaming, and do something mischievous in a flash: he might wipe everything off the table or quickly go and hit another child – he always chose the smaller, helpless ones who were therefore very afraid of him. He might turn on a light or a tap; or he would suddenly run away from his mother or the adult who was with him and be impossible to get back, or jump into puddles and make himself dirty all over' (p. 88).

Fritz displayed the physical clumsiness that Asperger emphasises in his description of autistic children; he refused to do gymnastics (he could not keep rhythm) and was also a challenge to teach. He found writing very difficult: the page was 'scrawled all over with huge sweeping strokes' (p. 94); the pencil he held in his tense hands pierced holes in the page, the words all ran together and were very badly spelt, although when required he could write them perfectly well. Despite being able to read fairly quickly, Fritz seemed to be totally indifferent to the other subjects being taught: 'he did not listen and would just get up to mischief. It was therefore especially surprising to discover on various chance occasions, for example from the mother's reports, that he had understood much of the subject matter and had assimilated it fairly well. It is in fact entirely characteristic of Fritz V and all other children of this type that they appear to see a great deal solely with their "peripheral vision", perceiving only "from the edge of attention", and yet they assimilate intellectual material. Both active and passive attention are significantly disturbed and they have great difficulty retrieving their knowledge – and yet they have, as is often only discovered by chance, an unusually rich inner life, a strong capacity for logical thinking and a particular aptitude for abstract thought' (pp. 94–95).

In fact, Fritz passed the formal examination for moving into the next class every year and although he could not be educated in an ordinary setting, by the third year of primary school he was still in a class with children of his own age.

The test situations are contradictory: although these were usually impossible to conduct because of the child's negativity, some responses showed superior abilities for his age, especially in arithmetic. His knowledge became particularly apparent in the individual specialised teaching that he received in the institution. Already able to calculate beyond 10 without any formal learning, he discovered fractions and their arithmetic by himself in his first year of school. More amazingly still, he had discovered negative numbers for himself and was using them in calculations (such as 3 – 5 = -2). At the end of this first year, he knew how to use the rule of three. Asperger concluded that, depending on the examiner or the circumstances 'this kind of person can quite justifiably be classified either as a child prodigy or an imbecile!' (p. 90).

However, Asperger qualifies Fritz's 'maliciousness', adding that he experienced genuine feelings for those who took care of him and sometimes responded to their affection: Fritz said that he very much liked the schoolmistress and he made some affectionate gestures towards a nurse.

Asperger then emphasises the importance of affective exchanges with those around him from birth in the child's normal development and the deep disturbance of their regulation in autism. The reactions – intolerance of signs of affection and praise, imperviousness to threats and the teacher's annoyance – are the opposite of those of a normal child. 'The teacher's emotion is usually a sensation that they enjoy with maliciously gleaming eyes and like to provoke – "I am so bad because you get cross so nicely", as one boy with this kind of disposition said to his schoolmistress' (p. 92). From this, Asperger draws some conclusions for educational theory that sound entirely contemporary: 'The first point is that every educational measure must be presented with "affect switched off"; the teacher must never get angry or lose his temper and he must also avoid trying to be "nice" or "child-focused". It is not enough here just to appear calm while raging inside – as would easily happen given these children's negativity and sophisticated malicious behaviour; the teacher must also truly remain perfectly calm and collected, and retain his inner self-control. Without imposing his personality on the child, he must give his instructions calmly and factually. If you listen to a child like this being taught for a while, you see how calmly and "naturally" everything occurs, as if everything were happening of its own accord and the child were being allowed to do as he liked. Nothing could be further from the truth. In reality, guiding these psychopathic children requires a special effort and concentration, a particular composure and inner confidence on the part of the teacher, none of which is easy to maintain!' (p. 92).

Asperger then notes how difficult the situation is for members of the family, who become involved in intense disputes when trying to reason with them. 'The parents in particular make the most effort with this – and tire themselves out in endless debates that never lead anywhere conclusive' (p. 93).

In contrast, Asperger gives the example of Fritz's schoolmistress; when he is humming, 'I don't want to do sums any more, I don't want to do sums any more', she calmly replies, 'No, you don't have to do sums any more' and carries on in the same calm tone of voice: 'How many...' (p. 93).

Asperger also makes the contrasting observation that children sometimes appear to be forced in an automaton-like way to obey impersonal, general orders that do not seem to be addressed to them personally, especially if these are issued monotonously and 'in a stereotypic way' (p. 93).

Finally, and this is a further dimension, he argues that the child has a genuine perception of the teacher's inner feelings: 'Surprising as this may seem, these children have an especially good feel for the teacher's personality. However difficult they are even under the most favourable educational conditions, they can in fact be guided and even taught by people who not only understand them but also are truly well-disposed towards them, and show them goodwill and some humour. The law of "thymogenic automatism" also applies to them: the teacher's instinctive behaviour and emotional attitude automatically (hence the term "thymogenic automatism") influence the child's mood and behaviour in an involuntary and unconscious way' (p. 93).

Hellmuth L

After a difficult delivery during which he had to be resuscitated, Helmut had three fits of convulsions over the next few days. Delayed in his development, he could not walk or speak until he was two years old, but then did so immediately 'like a grown-up' (p. 110). Having always been obese despite a strict diet, he seemed to have some endocrinal disturbances, since he had broad hips and plump breasts at the age of eleven years, and his testicles were undescended. However, the thyroid hormones and pituitary gland extracts had no effect.

He presented a major ligamentary hyperlaxity. Asperger comments how the child, with his slightly unattractive appearance that was accentuated by a small head and extreme clumsiness, surprised him with precious and disdainful language, including unusual terms and sometimes poetry. He particularly liked lyric poetry. His spelling was perfect but he was very poor at arithmetic. He 'tyrannised those around him with his pedantries' (p. 111).

Meticulously clean, he often washed his hands and had many rituals, and he was particularly preoccupied with getting dressed. He could be naughty with other children; when he was younger he would break things and then hide them, and his level of integration was almost nil. His mother had therefore decided to employ a private tutor after primary school. Asperger continues: 'He clearly has no inkling that he does not fit into this world, or he would not be so quick to show off in this way, especially not in front of other children. It is not surprising that he was always so badly teased by children or that they would run after him in the street and mock him – not least because he would become so thoroughly annoyed, immediately getting into a terrible rage, but of course could do no harm to the fleet-footed rascals, and only looked all the more ridiculous in his helpless fury' (p. 110).

Asperger concludes from this case that neonatal anoxia can produce similar symptoms to congenital autism, which he regards as connected with heredity. Interestingly, two of Hellmuth's physical symptoms – obesity and ligamentary hyperlaxity – in a three-year-old child whose behaviour appears to be autistic would today give rise to suspicions of Prader-Willi syndrome associated with a genetic anomaly. This would certainly have pleased Asperger, even if, on the one hand, I do not know whether the clinical profile would resemble Hellmuth at adolescence or whether, on the other, he is specifically presenting this case as an example of a neonatal cerebral traumatic aetiology that is non-hereditary.

Asperger's view of autistic symptoms

According to Asperger, the specific character traits appear at the age of two years and persist throughout life. Relational disturbance, of varying intensity, is a constant feature. There are specific interests, which vary according to the child concerned. However, the disturbance that hampers them in their relations as children is the same as that which will complicate their adult lives, with further consequences for everyday life and social adaptation.

When they are very young, children hardly ever fix their gaze on a person or a particular object and they show no capacity for 'lively attention and contact' (p. 112). Asperger emphasises the importance of the gaze in communication between mother and child before the age of three months. The gaze then remains an essential component of normal communication and forms the basis for non-verbal communication 'with the tone of voice, facial expression and gestures' (p. 113). 'Many of these exchanges therefore take place through the gaze, but this is of no interest to the relationally disturbed autistic child. He hardly looks at the person speaking to him, generally staring straight past him and, at most, casting him the occasional sidelong glance. It is entirely characteristic that these children do not look at anything with a firm and constant gaze but as if they could only see from their peripheral field of vision, and nevertheless that they are then, as becomes obvious on many occasions, able to perceive and process a great deal of the world around them. There is one kind of occasion, however, on which these children's gaze is capable of intense expression, which is when they have some malicious action in mind; then, their eyes flash, and the deed has already been done' (p. 113).

He then draws a parallel with language. Like the gaze, language carries expression, 'which is at least as important as its function of conveying factual information – all affects are predominantly expressed through language. Every aspect of the relationship between interlocutors – authority or subordination, sympathy or antipathy – is unmistakably expressed in the tone of their words – even when the content of the words is deceptive' (p. 113). Asperger notes that this is how we can tell if we are being lied to or not and what rings true or false. 'Again, we will not be surprised to find that these kinds of expressive manifestations by which contact is made are distorted in people with relational disturbances' (p. 114). As we have seen with Fritz, the tone, rhythm and melody of language are disturbed. Whether this is monotonous or exaggeratedly modulated language in the style of a bad declamation, in either case it sounds unnatural: 'It resembles a caricature and it evokes derision'. 'Furthermore, it is not addressed to a listener, but seems to be spoken almost into a void, just as the gaze usually does not meet and fix on the interlocutor but goes past him' (p. 114).

Autistic intelligence

Asperger was struck by the fact that autistic children do not learn like others – it is difficult for them to learn from the teacher – as well as by their original way of expressing what they know in comparison with the usual way in which children speak. 'Some examples: a boy aged between six and seven years old said the difference between a staircase and a ladder was that "the ladder goes into a point and the staircase goes round like a snake". Particularly rich in original linguistic productions was an eleven-year-old autistic boy, who said "I can do that in my head but not through my mouth" (meaning that he had understood something but could not express it), "my sleep today was long but thin" (also an example of autistic self-examination) ... When asked if he was religious, "I would not say that I am irreligious but I do not have any clear indication of God" ' (p. 115).

This originality of perspective, sometimes surprisingly mature, usually develops in a compartmentalised and hypertrophic way. Some children become amateur chemists and terrorise people around them with their experiments: one child, for example, had specialised in poisons and had stolen some potassium cyanate from school! Others, self-taught mathematicians, can have the greatest difficulty following the ordinary teaching in this field, and have to use their own methods, including for the simplest forms of learning. For instance, one autistic child could only add 5 and 6 by subtracting 1 from 12, since he could not accept automatic operations that were externally imposed.

Asperger also observes how remote from reality these specific interests often are. For example, a child with strong technical interests might design spaceships. However, he acknowledges that they show a maturity in the artistic field that is lacking in normal children, associating this quality with their egocentricity and a very certain judgement of other people. He also notes their attention to their perceptions: a child who feels homesick uses the following way of calming down: 'If you put your head on the pillow, then there is a rustling sound in your ear and then you have to lie there quietly for a long time and it is lovely' (p. 117).

Asperger wonders how it is that the principal anomaly in autistic children, the key to all the others, namely 'a disturbance in lively relations with those around them' (p. 117), can coexist with this perceptiveness about the environment that is sometimes so remarkable. He resolves the contradiction by emphasising the distance that is required for abstraction and gaining awareness. 'It is precisely this increased personal distance, the characteristically autistic disturbance in instinctive and emotional responses, that therefore in a certain sense provides the basis for their strong conceptual grasp of the world. This is why we refer to a "psychopathic perspicacity" in these children, because it occurs exclusively in them. In cases where this favourable disposition applies, this capacity ... becomes the foundation for exceptional achievements that are denied to others' (p. 118).

However, Asperger does not fall victim to the illusion to which his contribution has been restricted: genius is not the rule and the personalities range from those with 'originality bordering on genius to eccentrics who live in a world of their own and can barely function, to feeble-minded automaton-like individuals with the severest relational disturbances' (p. 118). He thus gives the example of the children who can calculate calendars or those who know all the tramlines in Vienna by heart.

With remarkable contemporary relevance, Asperger indicates the conflicts between parents and teachers; the former, judging their children by the spontaneous manifestations of their intelligence, consider them to be highly gifted, whereas the latter observe that they have difficulty learning and give them bad marks – 'providing ample grounds for conflict in which there is some right on both sides' (p. 120). Finally, he emphasises the inadequacy of intelligence tests that mainly measure capacities for abstraction and logic, which are perfect in a high-functioning autist, but underestimate disturbances in learning capacities.

Family and social life

Structured by the affective relationships between its members, the family is deeply disturbed by a child who rejects affection: 'For the parents, this unfeeling behaviour is particularly painful and they are especially unhappy in consequence' (p. 121). Returning to the negativity and 'malicious behaviour' – with inverted commas this time – of autistic children and their isolation, Asperger quotes the comment that is often made: 'It is as if he were alone in all the world' (p. 122) and then refers back to the stereotypies of their early years – 'rhythmic swaying, playing repetitively for hours on end with a shoelace or a particular toy that is treated almost like a fetish, such as a whip or an old doll. The children strike and beat things and clearly enjoy the rhythm, they set out their toys in rows, for example, or line up their bricks according to colour, shape or size or other unfathomable rules instead of building with them. It is usually impossible to tear them away from their play and their difficulties' (p. 122). He then gives the example of a child who had trouble eating because he was always staring endlessly at the fat globules, like 'living and expressive' eyes, in the soup that was served to him.

Affectivity and sexuality

Although it is sometimes almost entirely absent, Asperger emphasises the extravagant quality that usually characterises sexuality in autistic people. It mainly consists in masturbation, without shame or guilt, and this is sometimes exhibited. He also records homosexual behaviour in relatively young children. The sadistic dimension is present: an excited reaction to an injury received by their mother or, which surprises him even more, their own injuries. 'It would be so nice if I were a wolf, then I could tear sheep and people to pieces and blood would pour everywhere' (p. 124), as one child said.

In other domains of life, strange phobias, surprising likes and dislikes – bitter or highly seasoned dishes – reinforce this impression of conflicting drive impulses. Object relations are disturbed and the autistic child does not bring them alive in the way that other young children do. Autistic children categorise and collect miscellaneous objects and some later develop impressive obsessional collections. Humourlessness is a characteristic feature, except in connection with their creativity as it emerges in word play.

However, Asperger modifies this impressive picture by attesting to the despair felt by children who are separated from their families when they go to boarding schools. Some cry for days at a time in utter despair. Most of them, suddenly feeling their pain in the evening, 'talk about their parents whom they have caused so much trouble at home and about their homes in the most tender terms' (p. 127), demonstrating surprisingly sophisticated feelings better than other children of the same age. He concludes: 'In light of these facts, the problem of these children's emotional nature has become highly complex. It is in any case not easy to understand according to the concept of an "emotional deficit", thus in quantitative terms; it is much more a qualitatively different nature, with emotional and constitutional discrepancies and often with surprising contradictions, that characterises these children, giving rise to their adaptational difficulties' (p. 128).

What becomes of them?

Psychopaths have traditionally been described as people who both suffer and cause suffering to those around them. Asperger is certain that the second proposition applies to autistic psychopaths, but is unsure what to conclude about the first, given the impenetrable nature of their personalities. However, their social capacities can be fostered by their outstanding achievements, their tenacity and their narrow field of interests. The profession to which they devote themselves has to be derived from their spontaneous activities: 'This profession emerges from their particular disposition in a way that seems predestined' (p. 133).

A three-year-old boy asked his mother to draw him some shapes in the sand one day: a triangle, a rectangle and a pentagon. Taking a stick, he drew a line and said: 'This is a biangle', then he drew a point and said: 'And this is a uniangle?' (p. 134). Before he started at school, he had already discovered how to find a cubic root! As a result of his level in mathematics, despite some extraordinary gaps in other subjects, he passed his baccalaureate. At university, he discovered an error in Newton's calculations and he soon became an astronomer, obtaining his habilitation as a lecturer.

Asperger assures us that these are not exceptional cases and mentions an expert in heraldry – coats of arms – as well as a musician. The degree of specialisation that professional life imposes as a painful requirement on the normal individual is a starting premise for the autistic personality, which explains why these people have their own niche in society. He observes that these are sometimes the people who have given their teachers the most trouble and in relation to these unexpected successes he concludes: 'This gives us the right and the duty to make every effort for them with all our personal resources, for we believe that it is only the total commitment of the loving teacher that can produce results with such difficult people' (p. 135).

CHAPTER 2

Psychoanalysis and autism

The psychoanalytic understanding of autism

AS WE HAVE seen, for Margaret Mahler autism is distinguished from symbiotic psychosis by the negative hallucination of the mother and the world. Although this idea has continuing relevance, her other hypothesis of a normal autistic phase experienced by every child at which development is arrested in pathological autism has fallen from favour. Mahler qualified this by introducing the idea that active pathological defences were also at work. She put forward a genetic theory (in the sense of psychic genesis) of maturation that identified pathology as a fixation at normal stages of development. However, her interest in a happy symbiotic phase between mother and child remains productive for investigating psychic construction.

In the United Kingdom after the Second World War, D. W. Winnicott argued against Melanie Klein's theories, which postulated a very early violent and cruel form of psychic functioning that was akin to adult psychoses. This implied a child who very quickly acquired a *self* – an ego with an awareness of its identity – and who was capable of a psychic relationship with his objects (objects of love or hatred, internal representations of loved people). Klein thereby supposed the infant's psyche to be capable of efficacious primitive defence mechanisms, *projective identification* (projecting a disturbing part of the self into the other) and splitting the *self* and the object into good and bad parts. It was not until a second stage, the *depressive position*, that the child was thus able to recognise a complete person, and at the same time feel guilty about his hostility and experience a desire for reparation, opening the way to generosity and love.

For Winnicott, despite the valuable contribution of Kleinian theories to understanding many elements of the human condition and psychic characteristics of mental illness, this did not correspond to what he had learnt about the mother-infant relationship in his experience as a paediatrician. In his view, it was not devoid of wonderment and happiness, even if the cruelty of the child's impulses made him fear terrifying retaliations. Winnicott's work highlighted the importance of the environment in reassuring the child – he has not destroyed his mother and she has survived his drive-based attacks. He too describes a happy symbiosis that is indispensable not only for the child to acquire self-awareness but also to *create* his mother and the world. The mother's entire art then lies in knowing how to be there so that the child can *find* the object that he has the illusion of having created. The sharing of the illusion, followed by the appropriate balance of disillusionment that opens the way to external reality, enables the child to accede to shared communication as something self-evident. It can be observed here that Winnicott is explaining a stage that seems to be absent from autistic psychic construction: affective contact that enables exchange to occur.

Winnicott never put forward a theory of childhood autism because he considered it simply as an extreme form of infantile psychosis that deployed the same defences: he understood pronominal inversions (saying 'you' instead of 'I') as an extreme form of projective identification. As he explained in a conference paper written in 1967,[1] he refused to label a disorder in such a way as to suggest that it cannot evolve. For him, psychic pathology exists on a continuum.

It seems to me that here Winnicott is overestimating the projective capacities in autism, the absence of which was later emphasised by Meltzer. Moreover, I consider the distinction between autism and psychosis to be a useful one.

However, Winnicott helped us in a general way to challenge the idea of a child existing in our own image from the outset, with an inner self and awareness of a separate external world. For him, the baby does not exist as such; he only encounters a baby held by an attentive person, a mother-child unity. He postulates that in separations that are too abrupt or too prolonged for the child's capacities to maintain an internal representation of his mother or parental substitute, the child experiences a *primitive agony*, an *unthinkable anxiety* that, if it persists for too long, leaves an enduring impression in his psyche, not in the form of memories that are accessible to thought, however terrible, but as distortions in his psychic structuring. This explains the therapeutic value of regression in psychoanalytic treatment for enabling the patient not simply to receive what has been lacking but rather to revisit a catastrophe undergone at a time when the psyche had no means of feeling it without being destroyed in the process.

---

1 The aetiology of infantile schizophrenia in terms of adaptive failure. In *Thinking About Children* (pp. 218–230), ed. R. Shepherd et al. London: Karnac, 1996.

Winnicott also states that he mainly agrees with Bettelheim's ideas concerning the understanding of autistic retreat as an extremely rigid form of despair. However, for him this is a general model that gives an equally good account of profound but subtle personality disorders in some patients with neurotic symptoms.

Winnicott provides another fundamental concept for understanding autism from his study of psychic birth: there are states of psychic non-integration that differ from psychotic fears of disintegration. Not only are these experiences not necessarily painful but, in fact, they constitute the kernel of creativity in normal development.

During this period, W. R. Bion in turn embarked on an explanation of adult psychosis and adapted the Kleinian model to provide a better understanding of the psychic void in psychosis. He went on to describe non-thinking states characterised by the expulsion of psychic materials that cannot be metabolised (β-elements). This leads him to theorise that psychic birth requires a psychic *capacity for containment*, or a maternal *capacity for reverie*, which transforms the child's psychic fragments (bizarre objects) into α-elements, which the psychic apparatus can organise and experience emotionally. The child can then gradually take over this functioning, which he terms the 'α function' of transforming experience. It will be the psychoanalyst's task to provide in turn a function of this kind for his patient. Bion transforms psychoanalysis by giving it new parameters and unmasks the false self-evidence of the notion that an assured sense of identity and intact thinking capacities are universal. At the end of his life, Bion refocused his work on the importance of emotional truth in the psychic life of the patient and of the analyst.

Frances Tustin,[2] who was analysed by Bion, went on to concur in her own fashion with Winnicott's hypothesis of primitive agonies when she took autistic children into analysis in a way that demonstrated remarkable clinical intuition. She realised that her young patients experienced separation as if there were a continuity between mouth and nipple, since the child had not yet constructed the separation between internal and external. The experience is therefore that a part of the mouth is being *wrenched away* with the breast. This is followed by a catastrophic anxiety about endless falling, endless agony, since time has not yet been acquired either,

[2] Frances Tustin's books all relate to autism and the following have been published in French translation by Seuil: *Autism and Childhood Psychosis* (London, Hogarth, 1972); *Autistic States in Children* (London, Routledge, 1981); *Autistic Barriers in Neurotic Patients* (London, Karnac, 1986).

which she terms the 'black hole', adopting the term used by her young patient John, who referred to the mouth as the 'black hole with a nasty prick' (1972, p. 26).

Tustin described specific defences at work in autism. Unlike the transitional objects in normal development described by Winnicott, *autistic objects* are hard, sometimes metallic for example, and must embody sameness. Their loss plunges the child into his terrors, as if they were the safeguards of his own integrity. *Autistic shapes* are self-generated sensations that seem to envelop the child and insulate him from the outside world. These shapes can be bodily sensations, such as certain muscular contractions. Tustin emphasises the recourse to sensoriality that is detrimental to healthy forms of auto-erotism.

Tustin contrasts a rigid defensive organisation, the autism with a protective shell, classic Kannerian autism, with confusional, less structured, forms of autism, which can give the illusion of more exchanges but prove slower to develop because the organisation is less established. The interpretation seeks to identify the child's terrors and the defences by which he protects himself from them. The failure to open up to the other person in psychic construction does not indicate to Tustin a parental responsibility: as we have said, she describes Bettelheim's standpoint towards parents as 'both cruel and erroneous' (1986, p. 65).

While supervising psychotherapists who were treating autistic patients, Donald Meltzer,[3] who was also inspired by Bion, suggested adapting to this pathology a concept of Esther Bick's that denotes the early development of identity in the healthy baby: *adhesive identity*. This is a primitive identity shared by mother and baby, supported by a shared *psychic skin*, constituted from the mother's care – from the *holding*, the immersion in language, her smell and her psychic cathexis of the child. This stage therefore precedes any construction of a psychic boundary between inside and outside. Meltzer takes the view that in autism the child has not had access to the projective identification described by Klein and that he does not have any available concept of the interior of an object or a personal inner space. As the prisoner of a two-dimensional world, a surface that can only adhere to other surfaces, here again the child will experience separations as a wrench and a psychic death, since he exists only in the pathological *adhesive identification*. His means of defence against the pain is *dismantling*. The child passively splits, using the non-

---

3 Meltzer, D. et al. *Explorations in Autism: A Psycho-Analytical Study*. Perthshire: Clunie Press, 1975.

integration highly effectively according to the axes of his sensorial system. There is no more pain because there is no longer a psyche to feel it, and this terrible efficacy in the defence through psychic dissolution comes at a very high price: Meltzer refers to 'the loss of maturational mental lifetime which is replaced by autistic states proper' (1975, p. 16).

Studying temporality in autism, Meltzer once again draws a distinction between autism and the psychoses. In autism, time is oscillating or circular, as opposed to a time that already possesses an axis in psychosis, even if infantile delusional megalomania makes it a reversible time: the dead can return to life and self-engenderment and destruction prevail. It is only with the depressive position that time gains its irreversible trajectory, involving unavoidable mourning and renunciation, but at the same time hope, desire and any possible future.

I have discussed here the knowledge acquired by post-Kleinian psychoanalysts, which has helped me tremendously in gaining some insight into an inner world that is so strangely different from our own and that provides an explanation of many acutely alien and desperate clinical situations. It thus becomes easier to recognise the terrible suffering from which autistic people are protecting themselves, and consequently already to tolerate slightly better the shattering echo that it stirs in us as we share their lives and the tyranny that they are compelled to exercise over those around them. Moreover, and this makes it a genuinely analytic approach, this understanding undertakes to describe the defences at work in the child in his autistic state rather than to explain what he lacks in order to communicate normally. This also provides an opportunity to communicate to him this understanding of what is happening inside him. For anyone who might doubt this suffering, often denied for self-protective reasons in certain theories of autism, I recall the first words uttered by an autistic child being treated at the day hospital, and reported by his astounded parents: 'Help me!'

Some teams in France use a Lacanian theory that has placed an interesting emphasis on the specific difficulty that autistic people have in assuming a subject position. When young Don, described by Kanner, tells his mother: 'Say to Don: your siesta is over, come down now' instead of saying, 'I want to come down and find you in the sitting-room', he clearly demonstrates that there is no lack of verbal communication in his technique: he uses the imperative of an imperative, which is a fairly complex construction. He seems incapable, however, of becoming the subject of his wish or his loving impulse.

Similarly, it is worth examining the contribution that the mother's psychic apparatus makes to the structuring of the child's drives and language in Lacan's structural logic if we remember that the first language is always the mother tongue. However, there is then a major risk of abandoning this interpsychic structural logic in order to turn it into an aetiological theory that ascribes the principal contribution to the parental cathexis of the child. This is the *foreclosure* of the paternal signifier by a mother who imprisons her child in an *imaginary* relationship, in which the child's body is an object of *jouissance* beyond all *symbolic castration.*

It is possible then to misinterpret the early relations between parents and child, which in my view have enabled the child to remain alive, as the cause rather than the consequence of autism. Finally, the suffering of the parents, who do possess language, attracts attention in therapeutic interventions, which would be justified in terms of supporting them but not if the therapist considers them as the cause of the autism and the means of treating it: they are then placed in the position of patients without having been consulted for their opinions.

This criticism does not apply to the highly valuable early parent-child psychotherapies that work on the relationship with the child with the aid of the parents, without making them the sole vector of psychic construction. It seems to me that children who have benefited from this before they arrive at the day hospital have acquired language more often than others.

The psychoanalytic treatment of Daniel

When I first met Daniel, he was a very inhibited and frightened child, who avoided all contact and did not have the malicious capacities emphasised by Asperger. At four years old, he was mute, with a handsome face; he walked gracefully, rather slowly, and was not toilet-trained. His parents treated him rather like a baby and he accepted this contact with them. This African family had experienced some severe hardships before arriving in France, where Daniel had been born. He had therefore been given a French forename. Originating from one of the African regions ravaged by fratricidal wars, the parents had been sorely tested by this experience. Daniel's father had witnessed his own father dying of hunger in his arms in a prison camp that was similar to a concentration camp. As well as French, the parents spoke the language of their own parents' country of origin and that of the neighbouring country in which they had lived. They had been so traumatised by fears for their survival that material concerns were the priority when they arrived in France. They ran a small stall and had managed to obtain some one-room accommodation. In order to work, they had placed their child with a childminder for six months in the middle of his first year. When he came back home, Daniel was apathetic and no longer smiled. The conjugal situation had then deteriorated and when they arrived at the day hospital, the parents were no longer speaking to each other. The father was sleeping with his son on a mattress, leaving the bed to the mother.

Some time after he was admitted to the institution, I began to treat Daniel in psychotherapy four times a week. Within a few weeks, he was putting a lot into his sessions and was coming to them happily. I then observed that he was very sensitive to separations; for example, after the first summer holidays following his first year of treatment it took him nearly as long again to regain his confidence: it was not until the end of September that he returned to all the activities that he had been pursuing during his sessions before the holidays.

I had set aside a box of toys for him and at first he would just empty the toys out of the box by slowly dropping them one by one on to the floor or the table. Gradually, he began to choose the same kind of toys and, in particular, the colour pencils that I had naïvely imagined he might use for drawing. He dropped them one by one, which produced a kind of exotic rhythm that sometimes reminded me of the percussion instruments of his parents' country. Then he put them into a container, the cap of a toy milk-bottle in which he dexterously turned the pencils round before returning to his stereotypy.

In order to see the temporality at work in autism, we must picture the scenario five years later, when I was still seeing Daniel once a week after his departure from the day hospital at the age of eight for an establishment for older children, when Daniel entered my office happily for his session. He opened his drawer to take out his box, found all the pencils there and the cap, turned them round ... then, removing the pencils from the cap, dropped them one at a time with the same sound, which no longer conveyed to me the same poetic associations but the full scale of his dependence on this stereotypy.

However, I had struggled against this impression, and managed to use the pencils as a basis for exchanges and opening up. Deciding to work on the stereotypy during the session in order to join the child in a shared interest, I commented at length on what he was doing, talking about the colour of the pencils he chose, how similar some of them were in colour and their differences. Daniel reacted to this intrusion by speeding up his actions, which put a severe strain on what I was saying, turning it into something like a sports commentary! When a pencil fell down while Daniel had been bold enough to come on to my knees, I observed that he had to get down to look for it himself. Whereas a young child will happily throw a spoon down for his mother to pick up, as Winnicott has emphasised, Daniel did not entrust anyone with the task of preserving his only comforting possession.

One possible option would be to forbid the stereotypy in the session, but since for the rest of the day Daniel was being forcefully and healthily confronted with community life with the other children and encouraged to take part in activities by my colleagues I tried to work on the cathexis that the child was demonstrating in the session. However, I agreed to draw some pictures for him, write his name and outline some play sequences if he wanted to do these. Furthermore, although his father showed him a tender indulgence that kept him in the position of a baby, his mother was very exacting because she considered correction to be very important, and it was easy to imagine that this was a continual source of conflict.

Two pencils gave me some hope, but this was soon dashed. One day, a pencil rolled under a cupboard and I saw Daniel open the cupboard in order to find it! This was in vain because it was between the cupboard and the floor. However, this meant that he could conceive of an interior that might contain the vanished object. I showed him how I was retrieving it with another pencil. A few days later, the same thing happened, but Daniel made no attempt to recover it, as if he had only remembered the disappointment. More happily, I remember that when he opened the drawer next to his, Daniel captured in the box used in the consultation a wonderful sky-blue pencil that was missing from his set and, in every session for several weeks, he tried to get hold of this. A child who wants the pencil that he does not have and who wants the blue of the sky is revealing a very happy disposition and I decided to meet this with a calm but firm prohibition, saying a 'no!' that I hoped would enable him to install a possibility of encountering a prohibition in the treatment while also reinforcing his desire for conquest. Alas, there again he lost interest in the sky-blue pencil one day! I felt extremely sad.

Daniel had some other interests in his sessions: he would often bite the modelling clay and I tried to pay particular attention to the marks that his teeth left in it. I suggested to him that I mix some blocks of modelling clay and then produce some different shapes, which he then destroyed.

The inexorable repetition at work in autism is well illustrated by his use of the large Lego bricks that I had put in his toy box. He gradually stacked them up to build a tall tower, aligning only one of the sides of the different-sized Lego bricks. This reminded me of Geneviève Haag's observation concerning the child's cathexis of the right and left parts of the body, which I understand as a projection into the outermost surface of the body that results from an inability to project into the distance, depths or external objects, as in phobia. I was therefore interested by the asymmetrical structure of the pile of Lego bricks assembled, perfectly aligned on one side, crenellated on the other. As his pile got taller, Daniel surprised me again by dropping it on the floor from a very low height, as if adjusting a pick-axe handle by dropping the tool to make the blade fit the handle. In fact, the Lego bricks were then perfectly adjusted. This action became regular in his constantly identical constructions, and its ease and purity then evoked a timeless knowledge of the art of stacking Lego bricks, like an immemorial action of stacking millet.

In my view, the death drive at work in the autistic psyche manifests itself in a particularly pure way, without being fused with the life drive in the form of sadism – it is therefore progress when this occurs – through something that provokes boredom rather than aggression, and indifference rather than hatred, in the analyst's countertransference. What is fatal is erosion of the cathexis. I was thinking of using a metaphor with reference to erosion, but after seven years of treatment, Daniel was still taking his large Lego bricks as he had done as a four-year-old child, piling up a tall tower with a clearly rectilinear side and another crenellated one and, in an ancient gesture, adjusting them perfectly. However, the tower then crumbled, dismantling, to use Meltzer's term, on to the floor. By dint of repetition, my young patient had literally worn out the pins that fitted together and provided the binding.

In addition to the aridity that we must acknowledge, there are fortunately also some lively manifestations. From the first few weeks, this timid, withdrawn boy demonstrated a keen engagement in his sessions. He would get up from the end of the room into which I came to look for him, showing joy and affection when he came up to me. Keeping his distance, he sometimes demonstrated to me his interest in being distinguished from others in this way for a period in which I was concerned exclusively with him. Once he was alone in the room, he was initially much more reserved, confronted with a direct relationship with a human being whom he did not know well. He gradually overcame this, until he first climbed on to my knees, then explored my face, mouth and eyes with his hands at times. The most directly drive-related, oral, aspect was expressed in his taking my head in his hands, tilting it and, opening my mouth wide, trying to eat my forehead, as if he wanted to incorporate my whole head. I told him that he wanted to take my words and thoughts and my capacity for thinking inside him.

Some vocalisations, timid at first, turned into joyful and ferocious howls that embarrassed his mother on the metro! I was then hoping for a cathexis of language because there were some possible similarities with certain words that could be anticipated. However, this did not take place. Nevertheless, Daniel seemed to understand what was said to him, obeying some instructions in the three languages that were spoken to him. At the same time, and partly as a result of the institutional care in which he was having to try out community life, he became capable of some non-verbal communication, protecting a possession or expressing a wish. When he said goodbye to me, he used a strange stereotypic manual gesture and I was just wondering about this new stereotypy that only occurred at that time when one day instead of his mother a friend from the same ethnic group came to fetch him, and greeted me ceremoniously in the same manner! This was therefore an entirely appropriate custom.

The initially tragic family situation worsened and finally resulted in the parents separating in a highly conflictual atmosphere. Fearing violent behaviour from her husband, the mother telephoned us one day to tell us that she had left the family home and needed some time to make new arrangements. I suggested that she came to see her child at the day hospital when she could in order to reassure him. She arrived unannounced two weeks later, just at the beginning of one of his sessions. I invited her to come into the room that her son had rapidly entered and I told the child that his mother had arrived. To my great discomfort on her behalf, he did not turn round but took his box out from his drawer and began to take the toys out without paying the slightest attention to her. Dismayed at the effect that this apparent indifference might have on her, I suggested that she allowed her son some time to get used to her sudden reappearance by going to see our social worker whom she knew, whose office adjoined mine, during the session. She agreed, and her son and I could just hear her voice through the partition as she told my colleague about her difficult situation.

While Daniel was playing, I told him that I thought that the loss of his mother must have been so painful that he had erased it from his mind and that on seeing her again he was therefore feeling all this pain. At first, he did not respond, then after about ten minutes he let himself slide on to the floor and began to moan, then to writhe in pain on the floor while clutching his abdomen. It was in vain that I thought with good reason that my interpretation, which I repeated, was apposite; the physical and visceral quality of this *wrenching* pain was such that I could not also help thinking that the Trousseau hospital and its emergency surgery unit were not far away. I picked the little boy up and took him to find his mother in the next room: he was then able to rediscover his arms and make contact with her.

After she had been able to make new living arrangements, the mother took her child back and then took more and more sole responsibility for her son. Although we had made the same suggestions to the father so as to help him to stay in contact with his son and had gone to considerable trouble to explain to him why this mattered, he gradually withdrew from the treatment and also from the child's life, only taking him a few times, and starting a new life. It was as if he had not been able to move into another register of fatherhood, as the parent of a child who was growing up with a severely disabling illness, maintaining with his son his tender contact of the parent-baby type, which his psychic development and also its limitation, as well as his physical maturation, were making increasingly implausible. As unfortunately often occurs, the burden of responsibility for the child reverted essentially to his mother. I met her with her son once a month and I found these conversations very useful for talking with my young patient about his life. This also then confronted him with a triangular situation. Through his mother's tenacity and confidence, and in agreement with colleagues who had taken over from us in his institutional care after he was eight years old, we managed to conduct psychoanalytic treatment for several years. Daniel became toilet-trained during this period.

However, mother and child were not alone in the world with the dangers of a dual fusion. She obtained strong support from a community from her country of origin, which was united by their religious practice. She also showed me her trust and gratitude with some personal presents: the most touching of these was probably a magnificent deep-frozen duck.

Shortly after his treatment with me came to an end, Daniel was separated from his mother again for a small operation on a phimosis: he had to sleep alone at the hospital and she came to fetch him after the operation. She told me with great emotion that her son had come to find her this time, with tears of joy, looking at her properly.

If we assess Daniel's progress by comparing it with the skills of some autistic people, the results are certainly limited. Daniel is still mute, although he is trilingual in his comprehension. However, in terms of his social autonomy, he is now toilet-trained and able to live as part of a group while observing the rules of communal life. As concerns his psychic autonomy, he is capable of non-verbal communication, defending himself and expressing certain wishes. Above all, he is capable of showing his affection to those whom he loves. From this viewpoint, he is no longer autistic, and that is worth the trouble.

Daniel is being treated today by some other colleagues who have agreed to continue caring for him despite his lack of achievement, which is unfortunately all too rarely the case.

The point might be made here that the upheaval that Daniel experienced in his first year of childhood, the family traumas and the conjugal disagreements were not conducive to his psychic development, and this is probably true. Nevertheless, I would resist making this the basis for a simplistic aetiological theory that once again holds the family environment (and political conditions with a war verging on genocide) to account. We in fact found three physical anomalies in my young patient: a birthmark on a lower limb, an anomaly in his genital organs and an asymmetry in his limbs, which were reversed between his lower and upper body. This may also reveal an organic difficulty that impeded his psychic development.

Some testimonies from former autists

In recent years, some valuable testimonies have reached us from various parts of the world. Some formerly autistic people with unusual personalities have managed to emerge from their isolation and to give us access to their memories of their experiences as autistic children. They provide confirmation of some clinical intuitions, but also give us some new data in the incomparable light of first-hand experience, which give rise to some further questions.

Donna Williams: *Nobody Nowhere*

Donna Williams is Australian. The original title of her book *Nobody Nowhere* has been strangely translated into French as '*Si on me touche, je n'existe plus*' [If I am touched, I no longer exist].[4] However, the French title clearly emphasises the problematic of contact and its connection with the sense of existence. With a possible misunderstanding: if contact alone

---

4 *Nobody Nowhere*. New York, Times Books and London, Doubleday, 1992. French edition: Robert Laffont, 1992 and 'J'ai lu', 1993.

gives an adhesive sense of existence, then loss of contact is agony and this is why every new contact contains a threat of wrenching and has to be avoided. On her way through Paris, Donna Williams was interviewed by a journalist. This young woman who has managed to go to university must still have been experiencing some intense anxieties, because she asked for the interview to be conducted outside, afraid of staying in the office. This was despite the fact that the temperature was -3°C! Her self-expressive capacities leave no doubt as to the depths of the autism that she experienced in childhood.

Early childhood

The book opens with her first dream: 'I was moving through white, with no objects, just white. Bright spots of fluffy color surrounded me everywhere. I passed through them, and they passed through me. It was the sort of thing that made me laugh' (p. 3). She would generate the same dream while she was awake by frenetically rubbing her eyes, which invariably drew a slap from her mother.

If Asperger's young patients were diabolical, Donna Williams' recollection of her mother is positively witch-like! It is open to readers to wonder, if they wish, whether this was a contributory cause of her autism or alternatively the trigger for a hatred that made her emerge from it! The child herself initially only remembers her recourse to sensations and then receiving slaps; she does not refer to a person: 'I learned eventually to lose myself in anything I desired – the patterns on the wallpaper or the carpet, the sound of something over and over again, like the hollow thud I'd get from tapping my chin. Even people became no problem. Their words became a mumbling jumble, their voices a pattern of sounds. I could look through them until I wasn't there, and then, later, I learned to lose myself in them' (pp. 3–4). She then adds that answering with an echo enabled her to continue being 'happy losing myself' (p. 4).

What a testimony from inside the stereotypy of echolalia, with its toxicomanic quality … the problem lay in responding – to a world that was 'impatient, annoying, callous and unrelenting', Donna reacted by 'crying, squealing, ignoring [it], and running away' (p. 4).

She thinks that she understood her first sentence – her mother saying that she was 'still wetting herself' (p. 4) – because this made her feel ashamed. A phobia about toilets ensued and the child refrained as far as possible from using them, to the point of making herself ill. Food phobias appeared, as frequently in autism, and Donna explains them in all their strangeness. 'In fact I ate the things that I liked to look at and feel or that had nice associations for me more than anything else. Rabbits ate lettuce. I loved fluffy rabbits. I ate lettuce. I loved colored glass. Jelly was like that. I loved jelly' (p. 5). She also liked pieces of bread sprinkled with multi-coloured 'hundreds and thousands', as in her dream. If these connections formed in a 'true autist' seem incredible, what follows will be convincing enough: 'Like other children, I ate dirt and flowers and grass and bits of plastic. Unlike other children, I still ate flowers, grass, bark, and plastic when I was thirteen years old' (p. 5). Donna did not react to very loud noises, although she imitated everything, and she was thought to be deaf.

In a poem, she describes with hindsight how she perceived life and death as inextricable in her autistic universe.

' "The world" simply wasn't getting in.

I thought I felt a whisper through my soul,
Everything is *nothing, and nothing* is *everything.*
Death in life and life in death of falsity' (p. 5).

In a world full of enemies, she has some good memories only of her grandmother and grandfather, her father and her aunt Linda. She remembers her grandmother, with her camphor smell and her knitted garments with holes that she could put her fingers through in order to fall asleep safely. Is the autistic dimension giving way here to a genuine transitional quality? This is not very clear because she adds: 'For me, the people I liked were their things, and those things (or things like them) were my protection from the things I didn't like – other people' (p. 6). She then developed some symbolic rituals and objects to protect herself from bad people, thereby demonstrating projective mental capacities that are rare in autism.

Her father before she was three years old, who was unconnected for her with her father when she was slightly older, had managed to find her in her sensorial world: he brought her various fascinating trinkets about which he would tell marvellous stories and he would call each object by its own special name. Donna confides an inner precaution that she took: on her father's knee, she mentally added the ritual introduction from her story-telling record, in one sense mechanising it before listening to his story.

Her grandfather also showed her the game of liquid mercury balls that split apart and he gave each thing its own name. It was possible to have these exchanges through objects, and his granddaughter went to find him every morning. One day, she found him dead. She says she was only able to cry about this immense sorrow when she was 21 years old, not having understood until then that people did not die intentionally.

Donna says that her elder brother became her mother's only child. The father, however, neglected his son and his wife. She says that the names her parents gave her – Polly or Dolly – illustrated the family split. 'I became my mother's hell: she called me Dolly, the doll she never had. In her own words I learnt who I was: "You were my doll, and I was allowed to smash it", she told me over and over again' (p. 12). The quarrels between the parents and between the mother and daughter continued incessantly.

Donna did not hug anyone and no one hugged her, but she managed to establish some tender and sensual (that is her word) contact with her aunt when this aunt was brushing her hair and complimenting her. Donna continually played with her hair and touching other children's hair was the only possible form of contact with them for a long time.

Imaginary friends

Donna was afraid of going to sleep and would sleep with her eyes open, describing herself as a 'haunted' or 'haunting' child (p. 9) who was rather disturbing to other people.

She then turned to magical 'wisps' that she saw in the air and to an imaginary friend whom she called Willie.

I think that it is possible to see Donna's wisps, as I can, if you stop focusing your gaze and then perceive the influx of lachrymal fluid that covers your eyes. Willie will be more difficult because he is more hallucinatory, with his green eyes under the bed. Donna Williams has the subtle thought that his name derives from her own surname and his maliciousness, which she associates with her mother's malice, protected her from the maliciousness of the unknown world. This figure she has produced, which may be connected with projective identification, shows a capacity that is rarely attested in autism, particularly at the age of two years, as Donna explains it. She identified in fact with this hateful Willie in order to confront the external world: 'Willie stamped his foot, Willie spat when he didn't like things, but the look of hatred was the worst weapon and Donna paid the price' (p. 11).

As an adult, Donna is capable of feeling some pity for her mother and does not hold her responsible for her autism; however, she found criticisms of her mother very gratifying at the time. She even recognises an inverse causality: 'Though she was probably a social cripple before I was born, I accept my share of responsibility for making her one' (p. 12). She is also capable of subtly identifying with her mother in order to understand her. She describes her mother as the second daughter of a family of nine children, in which the eldest child had been favoured and had received the lion's share of the pretty clothes and dancing lessons. When her mother took Donna to dancing lessons, Donna understood her hopes: 'My mother was probably fantasizing about how much she had longed to be in my shoes when she was a child' (p. 13). However, Donna could not tolerate the bustle, intrusion and strain of the dancing lessons and, clenching her fists, she stamped her feet and spat on the floor. She was thrown out of the class. 'Ashamed, my mother's dreams and hopes exploded in her own face. I was looking at the floor. My arm was being tugged violently. I was looking up. Words poured out of her mouth, the tone was deadly. "That's it. You're going to a home".' (p. 14). This was a supreme threat that terrorised Donna. After this fiasco, she explains that her mother called her Marion, her own elder sister's name, and then changed it to *Maggots*!

Without making any connection, Donna then describes how she searched for another house, meaning another family. She would often swing on a tree in the park, hanging with her head on her knees, in a stereotypic swinging motion. A little girl called Carol, thinking she was doing a gymnastics exercise, with her nightie falling over her head, took her home to her mother, who washed off all the multi-coloured make-up she had put on her face. A happy alchemy of laughter enabled a relationship to blossom. Donna nevertheless gives a precise description of the encounter. The mother brought them something to drink and told her: 'You can drink it'. Donna did not understand. 'It was a sentence of words, a statement. I looked at the glass and at the mother and at the girl. The girl, sitting across the table, lifted her glass and drank. I was her mirror. I copied her' (p. 17).

What difficulty with the most basic of social interactions!

Donna was desperate to be taken back to the park; she kept thinking about Carol and wanted to live with her. She had taken the invitation literally to mean for ever, in the most autistic and adhesive way possible. However, she preserved from this a new identification, which supplanted Willie: attracted by the easy manner of her friend for one day, she secretly becomes Carol in order to meet other girls and to try to make friends with them. She continues to cling to the Carol identity despite having lost her, in a much more healthy process, albeit in all-or-nothing form, in a *false self*. From her clinging to Carol, the separation enabled her to wrench a 'Carol' identity from the other child. It is not she who has been torn apart. Finally, this borrowed personality also fits her aspiration for a blossoming of her femininity and for tender relations between mother and daughter. In this sense, it is genuine.

Donna Williams then impressively redefines self-mutilation: she pulls out her hair, hits and scratches herself for a period. She reveals to us that she identified her image in the mirror with Carol and desperately tried to find her again for four years! However, Donna-Carol would disappear as soon as she turned away from the mirror and, unlike Alice, she was never able to pass through the mirror to the other side. This reveals how far elaborated mental meanings can accompany the greatest disturbance of space and identity.

School

Donna was sent to a primary school, and we can imagine her as a strange pupil with no astounding achievements, but who liked letters, learnt words and had some difficulty writing. She found one or two friends to join in her 'mad' games and would escape to swing on the monkey bars or the uppermost branch of a tree! She indicates that she was able to read but used completely inappropriate intonation because she could only understand the meaning of the story from the pictures. In line with Asperger's observation, she could only calculate using her own methods of subtraction but, unlike autistic mathematicians, she did not understand divisions and fractions. She makes the interesting comment that she found the concrete illustrations more confusing than helpful. She would have liked to build things with the coloured counting rods that were designed to help with understanding arithmetic. She was therefore soon moved into a special class for children having difficulties.

A hidden meaning

In a new house into which her family had moved, Donna took over the attic and gave an interesting meaning to the very common activity of throwing objects out of the window – to which bars were soon added – an activity that is a nightmare for many parents of autistic children. 'As I struggled year after year trying to join "the world" and finding myself compelled to withdraw into my own, I'd stand at the window, pushing my face into the bars and dropping objects "to freedom," distraught if they landed in the gutter, yet glad because no one would see them and know what I felt. That summed up my dilemma really; everything was a double bind' (pp. 28–29).

I used to understand these concrete projections as an attempt to explore depth, an effort to project things in compensation for the lack of psychic projection. However, we have seen that Donna was capable of formidable psychological projections. She explains to us her identification with concrete objects and that her imprisonment was not a void: there is certainly a fortress, but it is not as empty as all that, to paraphrase the title of Bettelheim's famous book.[5] She describes it herself: 'Although words are symbols, it would be misleading to say that I did not understand symbols ... It was other people who did not understand the symbolism I used, and there was no way I could or was going to tell them what I meant' (p. 29) . She gives the example of holding two fingers together or curling up her toes. That 'had a meaning, usually to do with reassuring myself that I was in control and no one could reach me, wherever the hell I was. Sometimes it had to do with telling people how I felt, but it was so subtle it was often unnoticed or simply taken to be some new quirk that "mad Donna" had thought up' (p. 29).

What an expectation of understanding, which bears out Frances Tustin's clinical intuitions concerning *autistic shapes and objects* and above all the effort to understand what the child is feeling! Parents and psychotherapists are right in thinking that there is a person there to be understood, even if we are gaining a more accurate idea of the immense difficulty of this endeavour.

We are going to leave Donna now, as the story of how her life continued after the account of her childhood described here can be found in her book, which sheds valuable light on other children's behaviour from an inside perspective. Her own story is equally exciting, from her entry to university, her travels, up to her account – unique from a former autistic person to my knowledge – of a brief romantic and sexual encounter. She has also shown us some rare personal characteristics, which provides an opportune reminder of how different individuals who suffer from the same illness can be.

Temple Grandin

The other major testimony relating to childhood autism has been provided to us by Temple Grandin in *Emergence: Labeled Autistic*,[6] which appeared in 1986. Not only does she too have a great deal to teach us about her own experiences, but her personal developmental capacities enabled her to earn her living in a highly unusual field of expertise: the design of slaughterhouses. Furthermore, Temple Grandin carries out a study of

---

5 Bettelheim, B. *The Empty Fortress: Infantile Autism and the Birth of the Self.* New York, Free Press, 1967.

6 Arena Press, Warner Books Edition.

autism that establishes her as an expert, as is attested by her second book, *Thinking in Pictures*.

From the opening lines of her book, she takes issue with those who believe 'once autistic, always autistic'. 'To these people it is incomprehensible that the characteristics of autism can be modified and controlled. However, I feel strongly that I am living proof that they can. And this seems to be especially true of autistic children who have meaningful language skills before the age of five' (pp. 8-9). She accepts the North American idea of innate differences in the brain and hereditary transmission, commenting that her father had violent tantrums and a clear predisposition towards obsessional ideas. All her work thus strives both for recognition and understanding of the different ways of perceiving the world and to demonstrate their possibility for development.

Temple was the first-born daughter of a 19-year-old mother, who then had three more children. She was a quiet baby until the age of six months, when her mother realised that she tensed up when she picked her up. A few months later, she was clawing even at her mother 'like a trapped animal' (p. 23) in this situation, which her mother found discouraging, as she was unable to understand this rejection. This was followed by autistic symptoms: 'my fixation on spinning objects, my preference to be alone, destructive behavior, temper tantrums, inability to speak, sensitivity to sudden noises, appearance of deafness, and my intense interest in odors' (p. 24). She drew on the walls, played with her faeces and spread it everywhere, shouted at the slightest annoyance. She was diagnosed autistic when she was three years old, but was already saying some short words that meant something to her.

Like Donna Williams, she remembers having understood language long before she was able to produce sentences herself, communicating along a 'one-way street' (p. 25). She found the pointer used by her speech therapist terrifying, but she could not make her understand this. One day, when she was alone in the re-education room, the telephone rang and, finding the ringing intolerable, she picked up the receiver and said 'Hul-lo'.

Although she could produce some words – 'bah' for ball, 'ice', 'go', 'mine', 'no' – her voice was monotonous and she had great difficulty looking people in the eye. Like a scientist with a microscope, she would sometimes observe the grains of sand between her fingers at the beach or become absorbed in tracing a furrow in her skin with her finger, 'as if it were a road on a map' (p. 26). One of her first words – 'ice' – was uttered in tragic circumstances. When her mother was driving her to the speech therapist with her younger sister, a violent quarrel about putting on a blue velvet hat led to Temple trying to throw it out of the car window next to her mother. Her mother tried to catch it and lost control of the car, which hit the side of a lorry driving in the opposite direction. When the broken glass flew into the immobilised car, Temple shouted 'ice, ice'. She remembered every detail of the scene and that she was not at all afraid.

Temple Grandin emphasises that these words that emerge in states of high tension seem to break the barrier that usually puts an obstacle in the way. She is now aware that that helps to drive adults over the edge.

Again like Donna, Temple enjoyed spinning: it gave her a feeling of power and control over the world: 'Sometimes I made the world spin by twisting the swing in our backyard so that the chains would wind up. Then I'd sit there as the swing unwound, watching the sky and earth whirl' (p. 26). She also loved spinning a coin or a lid so that nothing else seemed to exist and no sound could reach her in her world. In the 'people world' (p. 29), however, noises are an intolerable attack. She still remembers the horror of the fog-horn on a family boat trip. Her family could not understand this and thought that she was a bad sailor. However, the governess realised that she could not bear loud noises and threatened to burst a paper bag under her nose in order to get some obedience! She also found the confusion of birthday parties intolerable.

The concept of an anomaly in perceiving stimuli seems relevant to Temple Grandin, who comments that today she can still get absorbed in reading in a crowded airport by shutting out all the surrounding noises but that she finds it almost impossible to make a phone call in a noisy environment. For her, to filter stimuli, autistic people 'have to make a choice of either self-stimulating like spinning, mutilating themselves, or escape into their inner world to screen out outside stimuli. Otherwise, they become overwhelmed with many simultaneous stimuli and react with temper tantrums, screaming, or other unacceptable behaviour' (pp. 28–29).

Her mother makes the subtle observation in her diary that at this stage Temple is more disturbed in the evenings than at the beginning of the day, as if tiredness were reducing her frustration tolerance. She adds that her daughter can also behave in strange ways when playing, which people find intriguing. She concludes: 'My beautiful child. "... when she is good, she is very, very good and when she is bad, she is horrid." I must say though, that even on her worst days, she is intelligent and exciting. Temple is fun to be with and a dear companion' (pp. 30–31).

At last! Finally, we find a loving mother! Parents reading this book may have wondered, from the painful descriptions of Asperger and Kanner, on the one hand, to Donna Williams' witch-like and helpless mother, on the other, whether the literature on autism might contain any testimony at all from parents who actually loved their child. However, the mother felt – as Bettelheim said – that she had been rejected by her baby, and the daughter describes her difficulty appreciating any tender contact as a broken thread of love. She was terrified by the affection of an overweight 'marshmallow' aunt: 'Her affection was like being swallowed by a whale' (p. 36). However, there was no annoyance on either side. All her life, Temple has been able to rely on her mother's unstinting support, even when they disagree, as we will see with her use of the 'squeeze machine'. As she gained independence, at first in a slightly enforced way for a holiday camp or boarding school, they stayed in touch, wrote to each other and never lost 'sight' of each other.

School

When she was five years old, Temple started at a nursery school with around fifteen children per class at primary level after her mother had prepared the way for her admission. She clearly relates the frustration she felt when her *associative* thinking was not understood. With the image of a bird in a garden, she paid more attention to the garden and did not recognise the 'b' sound of *bird*, but she could not explain this to the teacher. Instead, she ticked the picture of a suitcase, which she regarded as a sort of 'box', a container, beginning with the letter 'b'. She therefore got it all wrong because her logic was different and she found this intolerable: 'Frustration raged within me and I wanted to hit or kick to release the feeling' (p. 33).

As with Donna Williams, the slaps that she received in response hugely complicated her schooling in a normal environment, and she was finally expelled from the school having injured a fellow pupil by throwing a book at her face. She then had to attend a specialist boarding institution so that she could channel her violence through more appropriate responses.

At the intellectual level, however, it seems that unlike Donna, whose understanding of mathematics was hampered by concrete examples, for Temple these are absolutely essential. When a teacher took a piece of string to measure the circumference of a circle and showed that a small end of the string was left after having taken away three diameters, she understood the number π. She needed a concrete image to remember a symbol. It then became a gateway to it.

Another difficulty that is also mentioned by Asperger is the inability to follow a rhythm in time with other people or with music: 'Even now, as an adult, when people are clapping in time with the music at a concert, I have to follow the person sitting beside me. I can keep rhythm moderately well by myself, but it is extremely difficult to synchronize my rhythmic motions with other people or with a musical accompaniment' (p. 34). She relates this to the difficulty that she also experiences in trying to co-ordinate movement in different parts of her body, which may shed light on the clumsiness that Asperger emphasises. In any case, at school this resulted in her exclusion from these educational activities that the other children enjoyed. Similarly, her incapacity for rhythm meant that she was unable to write a poem.

The narcissistic sensitivity is well described by Temple, who joyfully remembers some reading lessons (half an hour a day) that her mother gave her, for on these occasions she made her 'feel grown-up by serving me tea' (although the drink was tea-flavoured hot water with lemon). I smile to think that now at the day hospital a highly autistic boy with oriental parents has persuaded one of our teachers to make him a 'coffee' in the same way while she drinks her own. 'She helped me educationally and raised my self-esteem' (p. 41), Temple observes.

Like Donna Williams, Temple is not always angelic. This is illustrated in the delightful episode in which, at the house of a friend who lives near the school-teacher, they both discovered some empty glass bottles and threw them at the teacher's house, wrecking the garden with broken glass. The next day, Temple managed to be hypocritical and to avenge herself on two boys who made fun of her by assuring the teacher, looking her straight in the eye, that she had seen these two children near her house ... And she watched them going to see the headmaster without an ounce of regret!

From the 'Rotor' to the squeeze machine

From her fourth year of primary school, Temple began to dream of a machine that would give her some pleasant bodily stimulation. 'In my imagination this wonderful machine would not be a substitute for Mother's hugs, but would be available at any time to soothe me' (p. 36). She understands her childhood dream as the intuition of a need for tactile stimulation to satisfy 'my damaged nervous system' (p. 36). She imagined a heated 'coffin-like box' (p. 38) with a plastic lining that she could inflate while controlling the pressure and that would squeeze her gently.

The extraordinary experience of the 'Rotor' machine at a fun-fair when she was 16 years old revealed to her a spinning experience that generated an intense pressure on her whole body from which she could not escape and that left her feeling extraordinarily calm. This machine is a kind of large barrel that pushes the riders to the side by centrifugal force so that they stick to the wall even when the floor of the barrel drops out (in the kind that I have tried out myself). There is therefore a pressure without external contact; the force of inertia that non-intrusively presses the body to the side comes from inside. This is a remarkable concrete physical illustration of the adhesion that Meltzer emphasises: the human being here is literally *stuck* to a surface! Temple finds the experience so powerful that she writes some letters to an imaginary friend she has invented (like Donna) 'from the Shadow' to require her school to build a Rotor to stop itself falling into the 'deep abyss of forever' (p. 81). The fantastical nature of the threats shows both Temple's liking for fantasy and science fiction and also some metaphysical anxieties akin to the *black hole* described by Tustin, from which the experience of the Rotor seems to give protection. She also says: 'The nerve attacks made me feel as if I were clinging to a greased rope suspended over an abyss' (p. 79).

Temple had another formative experience at her aunt's ranch, where she discovered the cattle and the work of the cowmen. She was particularly interested in the cattle chute in which the animals were immobilised in order to be branded, castrated and vaccinated. She understood their fear and observed how they calmed down when the pressure from the two V-shaped metal grills closed on the animal while supporting it. She noticed that touching the animal with her hand made it feel its own fear and that this seemed to have a calming effect. She stopped doing this and went on to experiment with the cattle chute herself by insistently asking her aunt to manipulate it for her. She finally felt the immense calming effect of the Rotor. From then on, she was constantly preoccupied with building a 'squeeze machine' to relieve her anxieties. The first models were lightly padded with plywood and a metal lever could be used to activate the two plates. As this gradually calmed her, she adjusted her prototype and added to it inflatable cushions that provided a constant pressure that she naturally controlled herself. She realised the similarity between the Rotor and the cattle chute: she even remembered having seen animals in chutes at the fun-fair when she climbed out of the Rotor.

The psychologists and the psychiatrist at the school were horrified by her first prototypes: is it 'the womb or a casket' (p. 99), one of them asked, laughing. Did she believe she was a cow? 'Do you think *you're* a cow?' Temple replied. She was suspected of sexual perversion. 'I had many fearful thoughts – some about sex' (p. 100). But she does not think that her fantasies came from the machine. 'Many times in the squeeze chute I had pleasurable sensations and thoughts about love' (p. 100). It is in any case noticeable that she seems to be engaged in something closer to the self-sensoriality described by Tustin than a perverse masochistic scenario involving a highly mentalised production.

Her parents were warned and put on their guard against this practice. This became one of the disagreements between Temple and her mother. It was her parents who gave way. 'Although the squeeze chute was just a mechanical device, it broke through my barrier of tactile defensiveness, and I felt the love and concern of these people and was able to express my feelings about myself and others. It was as if an accordion folding door had been shoved back revealing my emotions' (p. 100). She thinks that an initial very violent intrusion by the rotor was necessary for her to be able to move slowly from the hardness of the metal chute to the softness of the inflatable cushions. This reminds me of the difference between hard autistic objects and soft transitional objects. Her mother did not need me to make this connection. Responding to a letter in which Temple wonders if she is not 'just some weirdo with a crackpot idea', she writes: '*Be proud you are different. All bright people who have contributed to life have been different and found the path of life lonely ... don't worry about the cattle chute. It is a "comfy." Remember when you were little you rejected all "comfies"? You couldn't bear them. Your need to turn to the cattle chute now is natural*' (pp. 124–125).

Always skilfully advised by her teachers, Temple went on to channel her fixation into a scientific procedure as part of her degree in animal biology by studying modifications in the sensitivity of perceptions in the context of support with the aid of her chute (with some students who tested it).

Support: a substitute for containment?

It becomes obvious here how concrete containment or support seems to foster Temple Grandin's capacity to feel her sensations and emotions, and we have seen how for Bion psychic containment *by another psychic apparatus* was a condition of emotional psychic maturation. However, what psychoanalysts were not ready to contemplate was the need for a material device and a solitude that would allow absolute control. This may also explain the analgesic success of certain behavioural techniques that eliminate the relational aspect, which evidently gives them an alienating appearance to an outsider. It is worth remembering how much use psychiatry has made of enforced support over the centuries – the straitjacket, solitary confinement – in order to calm agitation. Of course, this is not really something that modern psychiatrists wish to preserve! However, the system invented by Temple is something that she has created against the advice of society and over which she has control: this profoundly alters the meaning of the experience.

I also remember the testimony of an analytic patient who had to wear an orthopaedic corset throughout her adolescence, with all the suffering this had entailed. However, she had realised, she had felt something was missing when it was removed from her.

Finally, some colleagues[7] have tried out the *pack* method with autistic patients with a degree of success. The child is wrapped in a humid iced cloth that covers his whole body (apart from the head) and blankets are added. The vasomotor reaction, with dilatation of the blood vessels, gives the child a feeling of warmth that comes from within. Less barbaric than these iced sheets make it appear, this is in fact an experience that seems to induce an enjoyable awareness of the body. However, we can observe that being tightly wrapped by the sheet rather than by a person is an important factor here. In this treatment setting, the nurse stands close to the child and talks to him.

Psychotherapy

Happily eclectic, Temple's parents sent their daughter to a psychotherapist before she reached puberty. She mainly remembers him letting her eat sweets during her sessions and that she ate a great many. She also says she concealed certain things from him because he sometimes talked with her mother when she was not there.

The chamber of illusion

At school one day, her psychology teacher, Mr Brooks, presented her with the challenge of building a chamber of illusion after showing the pupils a film about the Ames Distorted Room Illusion. This is a room with proportions that make it look as if someone standing on one side is twice as tall as someone standing on the other. This turned into a new fixation that occupied her for over a year. For the first six months, she tried to build a cardboard model and she had to improve her scientific knowledge. However, she could not understand the ambiguity of the illusion. 'Things are not always as they appear, Temple' (p. 91), another teacher, Mr Carlock, told her. This enraged her. Finally, Mr Brooks gave her a psychology book that contained the famous diagram. The following

[7] I have observed this treatment method in Dr. B. Cazenave's practice in Fort-de-France.

summer, however, she needed to build a 'distorted room' in plywood herself in order truly to overcome this problem, which was much more fundamental than it appeared, and to which we will later return.

Doors

As her mother points out to her, Temple needs concrete symbols. The religious metaphor of 'heaven's door' led her to spend many hours on the roof at two successive institutions or in a 'Crow's Nest', a roof window from which she meditated while contemplating the sky. The symbolic doorways that have to be passed through, the life changes that autistic people find so difficult, would always be materialised for her by images of literal doors to go through. One year after she obtained her degree in animal biology, Temple became obsessed by a large sliding glass door at the nearby supermarket. It opened automatically to allow supermarket visitors through and then closed equally automatically.

That door was permitted, used by thousands of shoppers every day, and Temple did not feel any excitement at transgressing a prohibition, as she did with her symbolic doors. However, she felt physically sick in front of this door, crossed it very quickly and stopped after getting through, as if she had overcome a serious danger. She reflects on this problem: 'I began to think about breaking the sliding glass door – put it out of *my* misery' (p. 122). Then she realises how significant it is that the door is transparent, because it has no hidden secrets, and she writes in her diary: 'It's just a glass door. But still it's a barrier. I guess the significance lies in the two seconds it takes to pass through it. Like changing from one mental state to another. No matter how many times I go back and forth I'm still in the same environment. But my perception of that environment changes. If a person changes his state of mind, he just changes it. The environment does not change. No mystery!' (p. 122). After three weeks of struggling with this, Temple can cross the sliding door normally and ... with a degree of satisfaction.

I am still very interested in the author's discussion of the changes in her mental state, particularly because we will see that the autist's awareness of his own mind has been the object of extensive studies. However, it seems to me that there are other hypotheses that may account for a phobia of this kind. The first is that the control mechanism is invisible and that Temple may find it impossible to represent mechanically and visually, given her dependence on visual representations. The second hypothesis is that the automatic opening without any contact, pressure or force may literally expose her to the impression of smashing a door open and the danger of falling, as with a tearing of the container that would ensure our safety. If the door opened on to an empty space, we would all feel the anxiety experienced by Temple. However, there is a third possibility.

Broken glass

In the seminar in which we were studying this text, a colleague[8] drew my attention to the fact that the word 'ice' appears several times in this book. She made the connection between this and the broken glass in the car accident and Temple's first word. Temple confirms her observation in this magnificent formulation of projective identification: 'I began to think about breaking the sliding glass door – put it out of *my* misery' (p. 122). To this we might add the episode in which she takes simultaneous revenge on the teacher and the two pupils at school by breaking glass against the house, spoiling the garden that was then filled with it just like her mother's car.

If this connection is relevant, it demonstrates an unconscious memory of trauma in Temple Grandin, which is fairly revolutionary because this would reveal a neurotic capacity in a former autist. In fact, it is almost a phobia about impulsion (the fear of committing an act of aggression despite oneself) that seems to underlie the phobia (the pathological fear) about going through the sliding glass door. A sense of guilt is undoubtedly also present, since Temple reports the episode of the car accident as 'the day I almost killed my mother and younger sister, Jean' (p. 21).

From the chute to the slaughterhouses

By returning to the ranch, Temple Grandin was able this time to begin to learn about the cowmen's work and to gain their esteem. The exciting documentary recently devoted to her on French television portrays her often dressed as a cowboy nowadays. She went on to invent devices for opening a door from a car with a mechanical time-delay and to suggest modifications to the cattle chute to reassure the animals. Gradually, she began to specialise in developing equipment for cattle, which led her to take an interest in slaughterhouses. Her first sight of them is strangely described, almost in a mystical way: 'I thought about the cattle I had handled in the cattle chute. They were being prepared for their final destiny at the great white plant. It all looked so neat – the white hospital-like building with a wooden ramp on one end, and trucks lined up at the loading docks

---

[8] Dr Bernadette Bonnet.

at the other end. I felt as if I were circling Vatican City and trying to figure out a way to get in. As I looked at Beefland, I hoped that the animals would not be defiled at the slaughterhouse. I hoped that they would be allowed to die with dignity and walk up the ramp instead of being beaten or dragged' (p. 129). She then developed a new obsession with going inside it: 'I had to face the thing all human beings fear – death – and try to find the meaning of life' (p. 130).

She succeeded in doing this, especially since she was not disturbed by animals dying. She is the most acceptable animal-rights advocate possible for slaughterhouse workers because the quality of the meat is better if the animal is not stressed. She therefore then designed some slaughterhouse equipment that provided a gentle end for the cattle. This introduced some curved shapes for the ramps so that the animal could not see what was coming next and act on its instinct to turn round. She explains in *Thinking in Pictures* how she sees the situation with a 'cow's eye view': she would remove a shiny chain that was bothering the animal or an iron plate on which their hooves would slide in a frightening way. She did not find the slaughter of the cattle painful because the death was instantaneous and she once again killed animals herself so as to experience the work of the slaughterhouse operatives in its setting. She visualises all her technical solutions in her mind before implementing them. She now only has to draw the plans. She proceeded to gain esteem in a tough professional environment, to which she now provides educational lectures on methods of treating cattle and their reactions.

Discussion

Sadism and perversion – Temple Grandin's testimony has been debated and Jacques Hochmann[9] put forward the hypothesis that she found a way out of autism through perversion in relation to her clinical approach to the extermination of animals. This is not a moral judgement but a diagnostic hypothesis of the psychic structure as it frees itself from autism. Geneviève Haag has thus testified to times of perverse organisation in the child then that are very trying for the therapist. In one sense, the way in which autistic people fetishize objects suggests that they are dealing with their deep existential anxieties (an object becomes the guarantor) in a fetishistic mode, whereas the fetishist uses his fetish to protect himself

[9] J. Hochmann, 'Arguments pour un dualisme méthodologique' [The case for methodological dualism], (1994) *Psychanalyses, neurosciences, cognitivismes. Débats de psychanalyse*, Paris, PUF, 1996.

from his anxiety about (what he perceives as) female castration. At the psychic level, a perverse organisation alone is often preferable to either autism or psychosis and it provides protection from these through internal splittings that allow a good adaptation to the social world.

Hochmann's hypothesis would explain Temple's social success despite her autistic anxieties about death in terms of their deflection as she herself becomes a cog in the machine that causes death.

Death and mysticism – In response to this, however, it might be said that although mystical emotion in a slaughterhouse is in fact rather rare – or certainly little reported – it may simply be that Temple Grandin has once again found a concrete way of dealing with a human problem where other people would find symbols appropriate. The catholic religion unites its followers around the representation of a crucifixion, a human sacrifice. In some populations, the drama of life and death is enacted through the ritual slaughter of a bull in a ring. Have those of us who have been moved on first entering a hospital as doctors not also secretly been trying to glimpse, to face, death ... in human beings in this case? And we, too, had the pretext that this was in order to overcome it. Temple Grandin would then merely be unveiling with autistic naïvety our general fascination with death, and dealing in her own way, as she says herself, with the human exploration of the meaning of life.

Regrettably, I have a less optimistic hypothesis than these, each of which is optimistic in a different way. I am afraid in fact that Temple Grandin has not remained sufficiently autistic to think there is no difference between us and the cattle that walk towards the slaughterhouse. In fact, we all die. It is important to her that this should be without a terrible suffering. Some autistic people talk about death as if they had a psychic experience of agony through autistic terrors in comparison with which death, as the end of life, counts for little. Our neurosis and repression have provided us with an unconscious that knows nothing about death and believes itself to be immortal, which gives rise to some misjudgements that are fairly damaging to the ordinary neurotic. However, what luxury in return in the need for eternity that we can share, in the creative illusion that we will continue. Temple Grandin does not want to marry, but she does not talk about children either. This also accords with her adhesive proximity to animals, which enables her to understand them so well: she strongly identifies with cows, as the cover of *Thinking in Pictures* (French edition) attests: she is placing her head tenderly next to a cow's head.

Sexuality

Whereas autistic people are often lacking in censorship, as an adult Temple is capable of genuine discretion and she remains reticent about her drives and erotic excitation. She had a painful experience of other adolescents' duplicity during her first visit to summer camp after puberty. Hearing the comment that she was not very interesting and had 'no boobs at all' (p. 50), she seized on this word that excited the boys and kept repeating it in her own way in order to appropriate it for herself, thereby appearing extremely sex-obsessed to the group leaders. One girl told her that boys had different sexual organs and 'advised' her to ask one of the boys when they were swimming to 'see his "peter"?' (p. 50). She did this clearly with no misgivings at all as to the other's malice, which is characteristic of autism. She then gained a widespread reputation as a pervert. She went to the infirmary because she contracted cystitis and an infection in her sexual organs required swabbing. Compulsive masturbation was suspected and her parents were asked to come and collect this overexcited girl who was disturbing all the others.

We have also seen that Temple was able to have sexual feelings and thoughts in her machine, fantasies that she states were not caused by the machine, which did however give her the opportunity for having those feelings and thoughts.

Finally, she explains very clearly that human feelings of love leave her feeling disconcerted like 'an anthropologist on Mars' (1996, p. 13). She has never been able to 'get' Romeo and Juliet – 'I never knew what they were up to' (p. 14). She had also never witnessed a disagreement between her parents.

Medication

Temple Grandin is convinced that autistic disorders are caused by biochemical anomalies and has been considerably helped by taking imipramine (Tofranil®) at a daily dosage of 50 mg. Full of common sense, she advises keeping to a moderate dose and against increasing the dosage in the event of an anxiety attack, as the episode usually goes away of its own accord without any increase in medication. She is very careful to avoid recommending her treatment to every autist, considering that others will react differently.

It should immediately be explained that imipramine is a conventional antidepressant (from the tricyclic category, like Anafranil®). Compensation for a metabolic disorder in the brain is as easy to envisage here as a testimony of autistic suffering. This latter hypothesis raises the question of how to determine whether Temple's progress has enabled a doctor to address her sadness instead of using sedatives alone as so often happens with symptoms of embarrassing agitation – in which case other autistic adults might benefit from trying out this prescription even if they are less capable of expressing their feelings – or whether Temple's exceptional psychic progress has enabled her to accede to a depressive problematic. This presupposes a good level of psychic maturation and access to feelings of guilt and concern, which is the case for her as we have seen from her account of the accident. In this latter case, antidepressants would only be effective for people who had attained this level of mental functioning.

Finally, at the risk of dashing the hopes of parents of autistic children, it should further be explained that American trials of antidepressant prescriptions in children, including new antidepressants that act on the metabolism of serotonin (such as Prozac®), have not demonstrated any efficacy.

Stereotypic behaviours and fixations

'Too many therapists and psychologically trained people believe that if the child is allowed to indulge his fixations, irreparable harm will be done. I do not believe this is true in all cases...fixations should not always be discouraged. They can be the means of communicating ... Turning a negative act into a positive one is possible' (pp. 113–114). This is the great humanistic lesson that emerges from Temple Grandin's testimony: you will help me by respecting my different nature. This is also instructive for therapists provided that it is accompanied by a shared interest. The teacher who encourages her to build the chamber of illusion follows her research and endeavours. He also refrains from holding rigidly to his own views, and he encourages her to learn mathematics and physics in order to carry out her plans. This is therefore not only a communication between one self and another but an interest in something that interests the child, which does not involve a complete (adhesive) clinging to her cathexis. It is another gaze. This reminds me that one of the early signs of autism is the deficit in *joint attention*, the young child's capacity to look at what the parent is looking at. This makes it easier to understand the therapeutic value of joint attention in reverse, when the adult takes an interest in something that is exciting the child.

This should not allow us to forget the risk of what Meltzer refers to as the 'loss of maturational mental lifetime which is replaced by autistic states proper' (1975, p. 16). It seems properly cautious to accede to Temple's plea only on two conditions; first, that the fixation is progredient, that the child is doing something with it rather than shutting himself away from the world and time; and, second, that this should be a means of accessing his world and following him into it.

Progress in understanding emotions and relationships

'Temple, the tone of your voice has improved. It's not flat' (p. 91), the estimable Mr Carlock tells her one day – he is the wonderful teacher who put his confidence in her projects by taking an interest in them and also gave her philosophy books to read. Only then does she understand how abnormal she must have appeared to other people.

Although Temple could not perceive the jealousy on an interlocutor's face at the beginning of her professional life, she learnt to decode social interactions much better – and she clearly explains that she uses a learnt strategy because this is still not intuitive for her. Ten years after her first book was published, Oliver Sacks[10] testifies to her development in his preface to *Thinking in Pictures*. She has gained recognition of her capabilities in the domain of animals but also in the field of autism, which is the subject of half her lectures. She can be humorous in her public lectures and tease him when he puts on the clothing required to begin the visit to a slaughterhouse.

Although certain emotions remain inaccessible to her, this is something that makes her sad. When talking to Sacks as she drives him back to the airport, she tells him: 'The mountains are pretty ... but they don't give me a special feeling, the feeling you seem to enjoy ... You look at the brook, the flowers, I see what great pleasure you get out of it. I'm denied that'. However, she genuinely communicates her sadness and her emotion before leaving him, suddenly faltering and weeping: 'I don't want my thoughts to die with me. I want to have done something ... I want to know that my life has meaning ... I'm talking about things at the very core of my existence' (1996, p. 15).

Sean Barron

Sean Barron's testimony is much more concise than the previous two. *There's a Boy in Here*[11] was written mostly by his mother, Judy. Sean too

---

[10] The famous psychiatrist and author of *The Man who Mistook his Wife for a Hat* (London, Duckworth, 1985).

[11] Simon & Schuster, 1992.

University of South Wales
Tel: 01443 668666

Borrowed Items 14/09/2017 14:29
XXXX1218

em Title	Due Date
olution-focused therapy ith children : harnessing amily strengths for ystemic change	21/09/2017
utism : debates and estimonies	21/09/2017
thical and philosophical spects of nursing hildren and young eople	21/09/2017
utism : identification, ducation and treatment	29/09/2017

hankyou for using this unit

hank you
iolch yn fawr

has developed tremendously. He is able to lead a professional life, and having initially wanted to take care of children, he gave this up to care for old people. His mother reports that he has a girlfriend, a car and some hobbies: he plays tennis and collects jazz records. His parents' testimony provides a valuable insight into what living with an autistic child can be like for the family and many traumatised parents will be able to identify with this account.

Early years

Right from the nursery, Sean screamed constantly. At two months old, while his parents were eating, he scaled the mesh sides of his playpen with his toes and dropped back down with a thud, 'crying desperately' (p. 8). It was impossible to take him on their laps while they were eating supper because he would flail about, crying. 'When we sat down to eat – our first time all day to talk, my first chance for adult conversation – we couldn't hear each other, couldn't think, couldn't swallow' (p. 8). The child always seemed to be tragically starving, despite the fact that he ate large amounts of food. At 14 months old, when his mother tried to show him a building game, in a flash Sean was using the table to catapult the objects all over the room, and repeated this incessantly with everything that came to hand, including the lamp. After a day of struggling and some totally futile smacking that did not make him glance at her even once, having shut her son in his bedroom, his mother remembers weeping in despair on her knees among the remnants of the lamp, at having hit her baby, and in terror because all her attempts to distract him had failed.

However, Sean's exciting contribution is that with hindsight he was able to explain what symptoms that were relentless and incomprehensible at the time had meant to him. Again, we discover that these had a meaning for the child, although his level of achievement was much lower than that of Donna or Temple and his lack of language made it even more impossible to guess.

His mother had observed that he would scratch the carpet with fascination for hours on end. Sean explains that an existential anxiety underlay his stereotypy. '*I remember lying on the floor picking at the carpet with my fingers. It's one of the first things I do remember. The feel of something that was not perfectly smooth was wrong to me – I picked at anything that did not have a solid surface. One rug in our house had many small ridges; by scratching them I could tell that* all *of the rug was the same, even if it looked different. I had to keep picking at it to be sure that the whole rug was the same, all of it. It must not change!*' (p. 15).

Here Sean Barron shows us how stereotypy is not only a toxicomanic form of self-stimulation – as when his mother discovers him paralysed by switching a light switch off and on. It can also be a constant struggle against anxiety about identity, its temporal duration – and thus existence itself: is the carpet the same in spite of its patterns?

The tyrannical child

As a young boy, Sean had a scientifically curious side that was absorbed in his investigations and he was very interested in holes, which he probed as if he were dropping a stone into a well to estimate its depth. A hole in the floor that went through to the cellar was therefore particularly interesting to him. Since the holes between the grills in the electric radiators also probably needed exploring, one day he dropped into them all the wax crayons that he possessed! The house smelt of wax for the next two years! He remembers this as follows: '*I* loved *throwing crayons down the registers. I was fascinated by the holes in the registers as well as by the darkness of the holes themselves. It was impossible for me to see where the openings led and how far down they went. I'd throw a crayon into the hole and then listen for the sound it made when it hit bottom. Sometimes I just loved looking through the register, so I'd stick my finger through the metal covering and reach in as far as I could. It made me mad that I couldn't lift the cover off and use my whole arm. The more I wondered where the passage went, the more mysterious it got. I absolutely* had *to know where the hole went, how big the tunnel was, and what the end of it looked like, but I was afraid I would never find out*' (p. 15).

The notion that he might be annoying his parents does not feature anywhere in his memories. Why does this child who cannot find his mother have the imperative need to find out where holes lead? Someone with a romantic turn of mind might regard this as an unfinished trace of the elaboration of the birth experience and Meltzer has discussed the hypothesis of prenatal mental experiences. However, it is so tempting for us to project our retrospective daydreams into scientific thought that I am wary here. It seems to me that the question of depth itself is being worked out, rather than a representative content that is occupying it. It might then be objected that that child has certainly acquired this dimension: he is therefore not confined to the two dimensions of adhesion, and this is true. However, it is as if the depth were bottomless for him, without any container that would enable him to master or to appropriate it for himself as a familiar space. In any case, it represented an urgency that was of prime importance for him.

The trial of strength between Sean and his mother frequently led her to hit him, although she had sworn never to hit her child: 'If I hit him hard enough he would sometimes look at me. I had to get through to him somehow, I thought, and if that's what it took, then I had to do it' (p. 18). However, Sean reacted only with incomprehension and anger, never with contrition, in the way already observed by Asperger. In a lucid and coherent way, his parents removed all the objects while clearly explaining the reason to him; but how could they remove the light switches?! They then tried to keep him firmly on his chair for a while after every stupid action. After countless further attempts, they had to admit that this approach had been a total failure.

This is what Sean remembers: '*I loved repetition. Every time I turned on a light I knew what would happen. When I flipped the switch, the light went on. It gave me a wonderful feeling of security because it was exactly the same each time ... People bothered me. I didn't know what they were for or what they would do to me. They were not always the same and I had no security with them at all. Even a person who was always nice to me might be different sometimes. Things didn't fit together to me with people. Even when I saw them a lot, they were still in pieces, and I couldn't connect them to anything*' (pp. 20–21). Sean suggests an idea that is new to me, which is that he also perceived living creatures as fragmented. The leitmotiv of the sameness that is essential for security returns, with the terrible recognition of the living creature's radical inability to stay the same. Paradoxically, the ritual of the psychoanalytic setting and the analyst's calm and neutral attitude turn out to be fairly well suited to providing some reassurance at this archaic level of anxiety: is this perhaps also latently at work in the analysis of neurotics? This might be regarded as one of the reasons for the calming aspects of the re-educative TEACCH methods. It is also partly why we have constructed a timetable that is identical from one week to the next at the day hospital.

The remainder of his testimony makes dispiriting reading for any parent who has felt rejected by his child: Sean seems not to have recognised his parents. He only paid attention to them when they thwarted his fascinations. '*I wasn't really aware of [my mother] unless she did something bad to me – like yelling or stopping me from doing what I wanted. She was not important*' (p. 21). He then says that he was unable to distinguish his mother from other women until he was six years old and he never really looked at her. From the sessions on the chair, he remembers words that he found meaningless and his rage at being interrupted when he '*wasn't doing anything wrong*' (p. 21).

This is a fairly grim statement, since we know that it is essential to distract the child from his world. How can we rescue a child while tolerating being denied? This is reminiscent of Bettelheim's idea as to the importance of how the parents tolerate their rejection by the child. To this is added the family rejection that is attested by Sean's parents and many others. Sean's grandmother managed to get her grandson to stop his behaviour in a way that was burdensome for her daughter: threatening him with being taken back to his parents' house!

Sean's first words, when he was two years old, were distinctly strange: in a shop, his parents heard a quiet voice saying: 'eleven-sixteen-thirty'. Sean had just read out the hour, minutes and seconds on the clock on the wall! Then he portrayed the position of the hands with the cutlery on the table and told the time that this represented. But he said nothing more.

When he was ill with a fever, Sean became calmer and more receptive to contact, and he seemed to discover his mother, but as soon as he was better he returned to his previous state. He seemed to be insensitive to pain and did not complain when he broke his arm, or when his fractured arm was being set before being put in plaster. On the other hand, he would utter loud 'ouches' while his mother was washing his hair, as if the pain were intolerable. How can this be explained? This confronts us with the coexistence of hypersensitivity and hyposensitivity. Is it that only his head was cathected by him as a place inside him? Are violent pains eliminated? We do not know.

In his memories, for a long time the birth of his younger sister represented for him the inexplicable presence in the house of a baby that no one came looking for. However, slightly later on, he became jealous and threw his sister's toys as well as his own into a tree in the garden, where they remained trapped. Exploring the higher branches, as well as the experience of the disappearance, was probably just as exciting as his previous exploration of depth, since the family was surprised in the autumn when a number of household objects that had mysteriously disappeared emerged in the tree as it shed its leaves on the lawn: an egg whisk, a shoe, a thermometer, a scarf, a light bulb in its box ... like Donna Williams, he had thrown his new toys into the bushes from his bedroom.

The experts

The psychiatrist who was consulted when Sean was five years old must have had his 'Bettelheim' side: he was so identified with children that the mother remembers him addressing her as 'mother'! In their obstacle course, these poor parents had previously received the suggestion of a neumoencephalogram from a neurologist who had only seen them for a few minutes. Nevertheless, the psychiatrist diagnosed autism and prescribed medication and re-education.

Sean was then given Ritalin®[12] (supposed to reduce hyperactivity and very fashionable in the United States) which calmed him for only three days, with one further calm week at a heavier dose, before he returned to his previous state. An exercise programme was drawn up and his mother was given the task of implementing this. This generally meant complete helplessness, barring some successes that gave her hope that was only shattered the next day, as if nothing had happened. One day, the mother dissolved in tears. She suddenly realised that her son was looking at her and then heard his voice addressing her: 'Mom?' I wrapped my arms around him and he touched my cheek, looking at the tears on his fingers. 'Cry?' he said, his face sad, open. His arm was around my shoulder and, briefly, he hugged me back. I held him for another moment, then he broke away and began turning the light switch on and off, his face blank. There's a real child in there, I thought. He's trapped and we've got to get him out' (p. 61).

There's a Boy in Here, the title of the book by Sean and Judy Barron, is undoubtedly the message that Judy would like to give to everyone who deals with autistic people. She has not suffered in vain in her efforts to find him. Sean himself reveals that he does not know why an achievement one day was of no help to him the next. He did not make any connection. It is as if the situation were entirely new and he did not think he would escape being scolded if he made a mistake. Exercise appeared to him as a further opportunity to be scolded or criticised. He does not comment on the emotion shared for the first time with his mother.

Sean could not tolerate a glass of water being put on the table in a restaurant: he would throw things around and explode in fury. One day, his mother forgot to explain this to the waitress and when some glasses of water appeared, disaster ensued. She talked about this to the re-educator who asked Sean why, as if he were going to provide the answer, which of course did not happen. Sean gives the answer much later: '*I had a rule about glasses of water when we went out to eat. To me water was tasteless, bland, not exciting. Therefore*, it should not be served with a

[12] Judy Barron later relates the nightmare of the Phenergan® prescription, which she thought was supposed to have a paradoxical effect of calming hyperactive children despite being a stimulant; this triggered an uncontrollable terrifying and exhausting excitation in her son. I wonder if she may not have reversed the two prescriptions in her memories. It is in fact Ritalin® that is similar to an amphetamine and Phenergan that is a sedative.

meal in a restaurant. *That was my rule. They had to serve something I liked – Coke, for instance. When they brought water and set it down, I got absolutely infuriated! It violated my rule and made me feel out of control and helpless. I knew the waitress or waiter was doing it on purpose to hurt me and make me helpless. I had to show them that my rule was not to be broken!*' (p. 67).

A tyrant hovering over the void

However, Sean's tyrannical behaviour can once again be explained by his fragility. When his mother describes how he very slowly overcame his fear of water at the swimming-pool, an experience that we also have at the day hospital, where it took one very anxious autistic child a year to be able to get into our paddling pool, he explains his fear: '*In the swimming pool I felt absolute terror. Even though I could feel the bottom of it one minute, I knew that I could be sucked under the next. I had no sense of permanence. I only knew that the pool could be bottomless and that it could kill me. I had to hold on, that was all there was to it. I needed 100 percent assurance that nothing bad would happen to me. The water itself was soothing, and I liked the physical sensation of it. But the thing was – if I let go, would there be a bottom to the pool anymore?*' (p. 76).

Here again is the anxiety about bottomless depths, very clearly explained as a mortal fear. In another passage, Sean explains that he cannot tolerate the floor with bare feet and he has to keep curling up his toes and rubbing the floor. Although other autistic people are always taking off their shoes, as if they only felt well when they went barefoot, this might account for the common autistic symptom of walking only on tiptoes. Is this not how we move along in water before we know how to swim? I was familiar with the idea that depth is only acquired by autistic people in the two-dimensional way described by Meltzer, but I had not translated this into the vertical plane and imagined that the ground could be so uncertain! This is another example of the self-evident phenomena that cease to apply in the autistic universe. Although I had been convinced by the 'black hole' and the fear of endless falling described by Tustin, I had not been able to imagine how the material perception of the ground underfoot could count for so little. Sean explains that he could only walk on the area around the swimming pool when it was wet and dark-coloured after he had been able to touch it with his hands. He connects this to the dark and his fear of dark-skinned faces or the psychologist's black beard (although not black people). '*When I was small, I used to have a lot of visions of something grabbing my feet and pulling me down, sucking me under. So when my mom and dad made me touch the wet cement with my hand, it didn't matter to me – it was feet that were vulnerable – very very vulnerable*' (p. 77).

This testimony supports Didier Houzel's description[13] of *precipitation anxiety* in autism. The term has troubled me slightly because of its active quality, whereas it seems to me that the endless fall here is a psychic disintegration. Sean Barron confirms this at a moment when the external reality that is already adequately perceived becomes the basis for this terror. It appears that a beginning of phobia, or external fear, has enabled the primitive terror to be projected externally. This may also explain the antecedents of certain phobias in neurotics.

Sean's progress is probably therefore due to this projective capacity, as we have already seen with Donna Williams: the terror can emerge from inside him and be projected on to the world, alleviating the utter confusion of the universe. However, this is at the cost of the child's terrors and the worst of roles for parents, who receive a large proportion of this projection of badness. This may be a source of some encouragement to parents and caregivers who are exhausted by the child's fears: the badness outside marks a beginning of splitting, of separation between internal and external and between good and bad, and thus a beginning of organisation of the universe. The nine-month-old child who is afraid of a stranger is organising that which is familiar, even if traces of this remain in later life in the fearsome human predisposition to racism.

A further indication of a projective mechanism separating good from bad is the fact that it is darkness in a white person that worries Sean, not someone completely dark in colour, as with the pale cement when it is darkened by the water. Is it coexisting contrasts that enforce or allow a different perceptual processing or changes that pose a threat to sameness?

The car journey back could sometimes be easy, sometimes terrible. With hindsight, Sean managed to provide the key to this unpredictability. He had memorised the map of the town and had also decided that 'a left turn was 'dumb' and a right turn was 'better' ' (p. 91). This is reminiscent of the splitting into two parts of the body described by Geneviève Haag. We use this spatial frame of reference in politics. But how could anyone have imagined that Sean was mentally counting the left-hand and right-hand turns and that he was rejecting the journeys that contained more

---

13 'Nouvelles approches psychopathologiques de l'autisme infantile' [New psychopathological perspectives on childhood autism], in *Nouveau Traité de psychiatrie de l'enfant et de l'adolescent*, Vol. 2. Ed. S. Lebovici, R. Diatkine, M. Soulé. Paris, PUF, 1997. This text provides a valuable overview of the various standpoints.

left-hand turns? His mother understood his unpredictable and dangerous tantrums in the car better on certain journeys!

Like Donna Williams, Sean provides the key to his food phobias: he would only eat simple food. 'I found them comforting and soothing. I didn't want to try anything new' (p. 96). He also explains his horror at different kinds of food being combined, which may be connected with our investigations into contrasts.

A secret erotic meaning

More surprisingly still – on one occasion, Sean started to run towards passing cars, trying to climb on to their running boards by clinging to the wing mirrors. It is easy to imagine how this terrified his parents! If I had been treating this child at that time, what possible explanations would I have considered for such dangerous behaviour? A suicidal impulse? A terroristic threat to ascertain whether his parents loved him? A complete obliviousness to space and danger?

The answer is even more surprising: Sean was absolutely intent on seeing the red needle of the car's speedometer on the dashboard. Obviously, this means the car has to be moving! However, the explanation for this whim is even more astounding. The red needle on the speedometer evoked for him a stylised picture hanging in the family house that depicted a naked man whose penis was represented by a red arrow! This is instructive for anyone who doubts the existence of sexual drives in autistic people. But I also remain astonished at the banality and ordinariness of the connection. I remember as a child leaning on the side window of sports cars to see the maximum speed displayed on the speedometer, which of course I imagined was what the car could reach. Admittedly, the cars had been stationary. However, the connection made by a small boy between a man's virility and the speedometer needle in his car seems fairly universal and persistent, judging by the fears of those who are responsible for road safety!

School

Sean Barron was accepted by the primary section of the school at which his father taught, which must have made life slightly easier. How he was able to accept even a limited amount of discipline remains a mystery to his mother. He referred to himself in the third person when giving his name and hardly answered any questions. However, he continued to pose questions about depth, holes or time. In a vengeful spirit of humour, she provides an enlightening testimony. 'It was clear that Sean was not an easy pupil. At the end of his first-grade year he was promoted, and we received a note from his teacher. It began, in lovely script, with an explanation of how difficult Sean had been to handle; then the handwriting began to deteriorate as she described his erratic and often disruptive behavior until, at the end of the note, we could barely decipher the final sentence. As far as we could tell, she wrote that she was leaving the teaching profession and taking early retirement' (p. 102).

How instructive this is on two levels: on the one hand, for anyone who thinks that an autistic child should receive no other treatment than his schooling, but also for anyone who, seeing a mother distraught in the depths of despair, attributes the child's state to hers! This gives an indication of the drastic assault on their capabilities that the child's autism makes on his parents, his caregivers and his teachers.

Sean remembers having been excited by dark colours at school because of the blackness they contained. His phobia about the dark had developed into interest, as with the water in the swimming pool, where with his father he had been able to overcome his terror in only one month. He also remembers being terrified of the children in the playground, realising with hindsight that this was accompanied by such a negative self-image that he thought that they were all children were going to despise and attack him, whereas this did not happen. This gives an indication of the vastness of the narcissistic fragility that is compensated by the tyrannical behaviour.

Like many skilful autistic people, he then developed a passion for geographical maps and then for the bus routes in the town – provided that the number 24 was not late in the queue, nor in the coloured marbles or cards that he then used to *represent* the school buses! He also memorised number-plates and then developed an interest in murder reports in the news: he felt he was as bad as the murderers and might become like them, since he was also unable to control himself, which horrified him. However, he secretly rejoiced at their fate: at least he was not in prison! This shows an interesting emergence of overt sadism, its counter-cathexis and the returning sadism when they were punished. I sometimes provoke a shocked reaction when I describe the appearance of a sadistic capacity in a child as a positive development (for him!). However, is taking an interest in crimes not a return to normality? Isn't this how the media satisfy their readers and viewers? Have you never read any detective novels?

If Sean had not been the first person to wake up and therefore get into the kitchen, a terrible temper tantrum would ensue. It was his younger sister who guessed that he had to be first in the kitchen and found an explanation for the tantrums. There again, he was able to explain with hindsight that he felt he had lost all control over the world if he was confronted with his helplessness right at the beginning of the day. This was therefore a total catastrophe. However, he tried to go back into his bedroom and to *pretend* to be the first to have got up. But the arguments with his mother put paid to the notion that the world observed his 'rules'. '*I tormented and teased Mom to get back at her, but our horrible relationship took its toll on me, too. Every time I teased her a disturbing realization came over me – I really could not control what I did*' (p. 110).

We can observe that our fragile tyrant remains in adhesive continuity with the world. His very integrity is threatened when the world escapes his control; it is his *self-world* as an entity that then breaks, as if our arms broke by moving independently. This is my understanding of the inner experience of that which I call tyranny, without any moral connotation, although for the family the tyranny as such is very real. Nevertheless, we observe that Sean is beginning to experience his hostility as a failure of self-control. A reflective quality has emerged; he is beginning to be able to question himself and he senses that other children on the bus do not have the same kind of relations with their families.

We will leave the reader to pursue the account of Sean's life for himself and to discover why a separation from his family finally became necessary. Sean was placed in a remedial boarding school for a year towards the end of primary school, then returned to his family. His mother tells of her constant sense of being accused, from reading *The Empty Fortress* to a family therapy that formed part of the treatment at the boarding school. During this separation, she also experienced the enjoyment of being able to be a mother who was available to her daughter and returning to work. Sean also described his first romantic feelings – despite also being capable of never speaking to one of the female teachers at the boarding school because she was 24 years old and he did not like the number 24 bus. The coexistence of normal feelings and autistic components is remarkably well described. He is therefore able to find a punch bag, but is taken over by a friendship with a child who shares his talent for nonsensical behaviour, which triggers a retreat.

Sean's secondary school years were painful, and he was subjected to bullying from his fellow pupils. His father also really cracked at last and told his son, 'You've been angry with me for fourteen years – now I'm going to be angry with you for the next fourteen years! I'm not talking to you *any more*!' (p. 187). After a week of silence, Sean believed him and was truly shaken. Their reconciliation sealed a change. It was not until the end of adolescence that Sean discovered that words could be used to communicate rather than to develop his obsessions.

One day with his family, Sean was watching a film about an autistic child whose mother was following him in his fascinations in order to join him, which was shattering for Sean's mother, who had struggled so hard against her child. Sean then asked his mother: '*Mom,' I said, 'I'm autistic too, aren't I?' – 'Yes,' she said. We sat very still and looked at each other for a long, long time. I had the strangest feeling, one that was entirely new to me. All at once I knew that I could ask Mom anything, say anything I wanted, and that it would be all right – she would understand me. Inside me a dam burst open. I knew I could use words like everybody else*' (p. 229).

This is a happy ending that is given material form by the shared achievement of the book a few years later, by which time Sean has made extraordinary progress in his relationships, with several girlfriends, and has been trying to compensate for the delay in his cultural learning by reading large numbers of books. We also note that one day when his mother is showing him the account of a behavioural treatment method for autism, with rewards and punishments, and wonders aloud if that might have helped her son, he replies: 'I really don't see how. I never gave a damn about rewards and punishments. There was nothing I *wanted* after all – certainly not a food reward – and what could you have taken away from me?' His mother nevertheless regrets having shouted, hit him and lost her temper. Sean reassures her: 'But you couldn't have allowed me just to do what I wanted ... If you had, I know for sure I would have stayed inside myself forever. With all the fighting and screaming going on, I knew someplace in my head that you were trying to get me out – and anyhow, it was the only time I listened!' (pp. 259–260).

CHAPTER 3

Cognitivism and autism

The cognitive theory of autism

JUST OVER TEN years ago, a development of the trend that presupposes an organic origin to autism spread to France from the United Kingdom. The inadequacy of behaviourism has led to a welcome revival of interest in what happens inside the human brain and mind. This trend is founded in an experimental psychology perspective that sets out to be scientific. *Cognitive* processes are therefore in fashion and many studies are devoted to them. Autism and the challenge it poses have therefore been a chosen field for exploring human cognitive functioning. Popularised in France by Uta Frith's book *Autism: Explaining the Enigma,*[1] these have much of interest to offer, although a rigorous debate is required and the consequences of their presuppositions warrant some severe criticisms. For the sake of clarity in this discussion, I shall first set out Uta Frith's work and reserve my critique for a second stage.

Uta Frith: Explaining the Enigma

The title of this book – explaining the enigma – is clearly less than modest and appears to claim that the enigma has been solved!

In an interesting historical perspective, the author reviews some cases of children and adults to which the diagnosis of autism would seem to apply. There is Victor, the feral child from Aveyron, Kaspar Hauser and the *Christian madmen* of ancient Russia, who were thought to be inspired by God, whose strange behaviour gave rise to interpretation. They often wore chains, which suggested that they sometimes had to be tied up. They did not observe any social rules, but those in power did not punish their extreme behaviour towards them. It is true that it must have been difficult to simulate this state, since they often went naked in Russia, well-known for its harsh winters!

Frith also describes to us Brother Juniper, the delightful disciple and

[1] Oxford, Blackwell, 1989. Published in French as *L'Énigme de l'autisme*, Paris, Odile Jacob, 1992.

companion of St Francis. He was so pure in heart that he took the precepts in the Gospels literally. He sometimes returned to the convent naked, having given his clothes to the poor. One day when one of his fellow brothers was moaning, demanding a nice pig's trotter to eat, which he was certain would cure him, Brother Juniper went and cut off a trotter from a pig that lived on a neighbouring farm and prepared it for the patient. When the farmer arrived, wanting to do the same thing to the holy men, there was great trouble. The monk undertook to explain the good foundations of the charity that the pig owed to his human brother with such good conscience and tenacity that the peasant, overcome by his sincerity, finally killed his pig and offered it to the monastery as an act of penitence for his anger! Uta Frith thus nicely emphasises what she regards as the essential autistic trait of understanding a communication literally, and also introduces us to the concept of a disarming naïvety through the total lack of duplicity.

Frith also examines some fictional stories and characters, from the sleep of *Sleeping Beauty* to Tommy, the hero in the rock opera of *The Who*; despite apparently being deaf, mute and blind, he plays pinball diabolically well.

Frith's view that early diagnosis is impossible

Basing this on studies of a large number of children, Frith shows that none of those who had attracted the attention of paediatricians during their first year later turned out to be suffering from autism. Moreover, half the parents of autistic children did not remember anything particularly unusual from their first year of life. From this she concludes: 'The relatively late manifestation of the critical features of Autism, as well as the dubious significance of poor social contact in early infancy, suggests that autistic children suffer from a deficiency in a particular mental capacity that in normal development does not mature until the end of infancy. This, then, is an important clue in our pursuit of an answer to the riddle of Autism' (pp. 66–67).

Aetiology

The author argues vigorously against the idea that autism might have a psychogenic origin: 'some people still believe that there is a simple answer that can explain, cure and prevent Autism: Autism is caused by psychodynamic conflicts between mother and child, or by some extreme existential anxiety suffered by the child, and is cured by resolving the original conflicts. Despite lack of evidence, this erroneous belief lingers on. It lingers on together with the belief that one can die of a "broken heart", or be made ill by the "evil eye". It is actually impossible for a child to become autistic because it was not loved sufficiently by its mother or because it feels threatened in its very life and identity' (p. 68). This sentence is quoted by Judy Barron at the end of her own book.

For Frith, autism 'undoubtedly ... has a biological cause and is the consequence of organic dysfunction' (p. 68). In evidence of this, she adduces the fact that one third of autistic adolescents suffers from epilepsy and she considers stereotypies, anomalies on the electro-encephalogram, the persistence of infantile reflexes and abnormal nystagmus (ocular motor reflex) to be neurological signs. Apart from what she states is an anomaly in the cerebellum discovered by Courchesne, she acknowledges that the study of brain abnormalities in autistic people has not demonstrated any specific anomaly.

Having mentioned neurotransmitters as a line of enquiry, Frith turns to deficiencies in genetic programming. She finds the strongest evidence of this in a study by Folstein and Rutter on 21 pairs of twins, in which at least one was autistic. The study reveals a very substantial increase (4 out of 11) in the concordance rate in identical twins, as against nil in the non-identical twins. However, she is even more interested in the fact that in 82% of the identical twins and 10% of the non-identical twins, the sufferer's twin presented some intellectual and linguistic deficiencies. From this she infers a more general disturbance in cognitive development that is likely to be genetically determined. She then examines the perinatal causes of brain lesions and the possible viral infections.

There are therefore many possible contributory factors to the autistic condition, but the fact that autism occurs in children who are not mentally retarded seems to Frith to prove that there may be a selective impact.

Weak central coherence engenders *detachment and fragmentation*

The study of intelligence testing shows that autistic children perform as well as or better than normal children in tests such as the Koh cubes, which are based on abstract geometrical shapes. They also tend to excel at finding geometrical shapes hidden in a complex representational picture. Moving felicitously away from all the theories of autism as a peripheral sensory deficit, Frith proposes introducing the notion of *weak central coherence* in the autistic child. This makes him detached from the general shape of the image and he succeeds better with the hidden images. She forms the hypothesis that he therefore inhabits 'an incoherent world of fragmented experience' (p. 98). She observes that: 'In the normal cognitive system there is a built-in propensity to form coherence over as wide a range of stimuli as possible, and to generalize over as wide a range of contexts as possible. It is this drive that results in grand systems of thought, and ultimately in the world's great religions. It is this capacity for coherence that is diminished in autistic children. As a result, their information-processing systems, like their very beings, are characterized by detachment' (p. 100).

It is worth emphasising this *central cohesive force,* which allows *generalisation* and cultural creations, as well as the *detachment* that affects the autist's inner being, in which it is said to be lacking.

For Frith, this detachment accounts for the fragmentation of autistic experience and stereotypies, as well as the incoherence of autistic perceptions. Always nicely inspired in her quotations, she illustrates this with a sentence from a novel by Borges about *Funes*, his hero: 'It bothered him that a dog seen at 3.14 (seen from the side) should have the same name as the dog seen at 3.15 (seen from the front)' (p. 104). This also explains why autistic people are often so good at puzzles, seemingly indifferent to the final picture that eliminates the design of each piece.

As concerns stereotypies and self-mutilation, Frith likes to think that in this 'distressing problem' the child has a reduced sensitivity to pain and is seeking a 'sensory stimulation not interpreted as pain' (p. 113). She refers back to behavioural methods of reward and punishment within set boundaries, which appear to have had some success in reducing self-mutilation. She also considers the possibility that stereotypies manifest themselves in autistic people because of their lack of social inhibition, whereas in normal people repetitive movements are reduced in the presence of others, but confronted with the inadequacy of this explanation for the intensity of autistic stereotypies, she suggests a dysfunction in the dopaminergic system, with reference to some experiments conducted on animals.

Finally, for Frith repetition still stems from fragmentation and the lack of a generalising connection, leaving free rein to the processes that govern peripheral perceptions – inputs – in a primitive mode that has not been superseded by a more complex organisation, and to a rigidity that characterises a more primitive evolutionary state of the species.

Verbal communication

In their verbal exchanges, autistic people reveal their literal understanding and the non-pragmatic quality of their communication, for example: 'Can you pass me the salt?' – 'Yes'.

Frith examines echolalia (repetition of the phrase heard) and she remains perplexed as to its meaning and the behaviour to adopt in the child's interest, and notes the repetition of phrases heard previously (as Kanner had done): 'Don't throw the dog out of the window!' had been said to a child during the previous holidays about ... a cuddly toy. Is this simply stereotyped repetition devoid of any communicative wish? Does it convey acceptance as opposed to a request? Not knowing, she makes recourse again to *detachment* in order to introduce the idea that peripheral information-processing systems are short-circuited, without the intervention of the central thought processes. The child thus only demonstrates having received the message by stating it in any way at all, literally, without incorporating its meaning: 'Say hello, Bob!' – 'Say hello, Bob' (p. 123).

Frith argues against the idea that there is any defensive avoidance involved in the difficulty autistic people have saying 'I' and their use of 'you' instead, as with the absence of possessive pronouns. For her, this only conveys a deficiency in understanding and using the roles of speaker and listener.

Commenting on the autistic child's loneliness, Frith links this with the maladjustment to communicative codes between human beings, and gives some fine social examples. However, she rejects the idea that contact is actively avoided, for example in the gaze. Quoting Beate Hermelin's experimental work, which concludes that the autistic child has a reduced level of general and non-specific interest, she takes up one conclusion drawn by this author: 'The child looks equally little at the filing cabinet as at the psychiatrist. However, it is the psychiatrist who complains' (p. 143). For Frith, these experiments conclusively refute the myth of a defence at work in autism – we will see that this is debatable – and establish instead that the anomaly consists in autistic people not using the gaze to communicate: the defence is replaced by a deficiency.

Joint attention

Although for Frith, some autistic children display a reaction when their mother leaves and comes back, which shows they are capable of attachment, she nevertheless identifies a specific disturbance in *joint attention* and *pointing*, as in pointing the finger at an object in order to indicate it to someone else. Thus, a normal child will point his finger at an object if he wants to know what it is called or when he knows that someone else will understand why he is interested in it. For example, pointing at a cuddly toy in a shop window that looks like his own is equivalent to inviting his interlocutor to share a mental state. His mother might then reply, for example, 'Yes, you have a penguin just like that one' (p. 147).

Joint attention can involve nothing more than exchanging looks. Frith attributes the absence of this type of exchange in autism to the ignorance that other people have separate thoughts: there is therefore no need to explain what you are thinking to the other person, since the question does not even arise. Here Frith approaches her solution: the autistic person recognises individuals and can become attached to them, but he does not understand the need to communicate his mental states.

Hobson's hypothesis about understanding emotions and its refutation

Peter Hobson demonstrated that some autistic children from around 13 years of age experienced immense difficulty in correctly interpreting emotions from facial expressions: happiness, sadness, anger and fear. Hobson then re-examined one of Kanner's hypotheses concerning autists' incapacity to establish an early affective bond with their mothers, taking the view that there is an innate disturbance in affect recognition. Although Hobson's work gives due recognition to affects and is of interest to psychoanalysts, it completely undermines Frith's specifically cognitive premise and the idea that the disorder manifests at a secondary stage, and Frith therefore rejects it in a slightly clumsy way: 'Such a profound failure can be explained if we hypothesize that autistic children have a poor conception of feeling states because they have a poor conception of all mental states. For this reason the effects that feelings have and the way they can be expressed in voice, face and gesture would remain a closed book. If interpreted in this way, the impairment in emotion recognition is not irreducible, but can be seen as part of a more general cognitive deficit in recognizing mental states' (p. 149).

Then seeking arguments in favour of emotional expression in autistic people in order to contradict Hobson, Frith refers to Derek Ricks' research into pre-verbal reactions in normal and autistic children to simple situations: their mother appearing in the morning, food preparation, frustration, seeing a ball or sparks flying from a magic candle. Parents had to try to identify the situations that had given rise to the recordings and whether it was their own child that they were hearing. Most interestingly, the parents of normal children identified the situations correctly but were mistaken about their child, which suggests that there was something universal about their responses. By contrast, the parents of autistic children correctly identified their children and were the only ones to recognise the situation to which they were reacting. Contrary to Frith's view, this experiment seems to correspond more closely to Hobson's hypothesis than her own!

Although Frith needs to recognise expressions of affect, even, she adds, a capacity for sympathy in autists, she goes on to demonstrate what she regards as the essential characteristic of autism, namely the incapacity for empathy and simulation. Thus a child may cry because he has hurt himself, and an autistic child can also express his pain, but he will not be able to cry without being hurt in order to get someone to pay attention to him, whereas any normal child is capable of doing this.

Gestural communication

Frith draws a clear distinction between *the hand as a tool*, in which the child grabs the adult's hand in order to get a particular task done – a phenomenon already described by Itard with Victor, as she rightly reminds us – and joint attention and pointing. Gestures are purely functional and some simple gestures are understood. However, autistic people hardly ever use them between themselves. By contrast, expressive gestures are lacking and again this is connected with the difficulty of processing mental states.

Thinking about other minds

The author's essential contribution consists in her application of works on *theory of mind* to childhood autism. Frith explains her choice of Georges de la Tour's picture of *The Cheat with the Ace of Diamonds* for the cover of her book, which I initially found highly disconcerting because it represents something completely alien to autism. This is because it specifically portrays the feats by which human beings can ascertain that another person has a separate mind from their own. The card-player does not know what we are thinking and we can therefore play with him, which would be impossible if he knew everything we were thinking. We can either cheat or not, connive with a third party or suspect the other person of doing likewise. As we are confronted with La Tour's picture, Frith reveals to us the ways in which we attribute mental states and intentions to each protagonist and she clearly shows how this is intrinsic to the human mind, which is a condemnation of behaviourism with its artificial endeavour to remove all intentionality. We can only agree with her here! For her, this is all that autistic people lack, as 'natural behaviourists', who 'do not feel the normal compulsion to weave together mind and behaviour for the sake of coherence' (p. 156).

The Sally-Anne experiment (pp. 158–161) provides a demonstration of the lack of a theory of mind in autistic children, compared here with some younger normal children and some Down syndrome children with the same level of achievement in certain tests, indicating a mental age of more than three years old. This experiment is referred to in works by Wimmer and Permer in the research conducted by Simon Baron-Cohen, Uta Frith and Alan Leslie.

A child is presented with a scene with some characters. Sally has a basket and Anne has a box. Sally also has a marble, which she puts into her basket before leaving the room. Anne takes the marble out of Sally's basket and hides it in her box. Sally comes back and wants to play with her marble. The child is then asked: 'Where will Sally look for her marble?' Most of the non-autistic children gave the correct answer ('in the basket'), already amused by the trick Anne has played on poor Sally. All but a few of the autistic children pointed to the box that they knew contained the marble. They therefore did not have a theory of Sally's mind as existing separately from their own.

This crucial experiment is confirmed by others in which, for example, a pencil is hidden in a Smarties tube – something familiar to all British children – before it is given to a child. There too the autistic children mostly (15 out of 21) said that this child would say 'a pencil' if asked what that tube contained. However, they remembered having themselves thought that the tube contained Smarties before finding the pencil. The Sally-Anne experiment was also conducted using real people in order to eliminate any artificial element connected with the use of dolls. It seems that Frith is reinventing psychodrama here!

Frith regards this fundamental disturbance in autistic thought as the explanation for the lack of empathy concerning other people's mental states and its consequences for affective communication. It is particularly detrimental in any situation that contains any ambivalence or ambiguity. Self-awareness is severely compromised by the lack of secrecy and the incapacity for awareness of the other's mind.

Pretence: a triumph of decoupling

Leslie regards the capacity for pretence as the precursor of the capacity to conceive of other minds because it uses the same forms of reasoning.

At around one year of age, the child, in Leslie's view able from birth to conceive of space, time and causality – which strikes me as rather naïvely optimistic – accedes to *meta-representations*, which are representations of representations, for example, 'knowing that you know'. According to Leslie, a fundamental mechanism, the *decoupler*, underlies the capacity for pretence and the use of meta-representations. Frith appositely emphasises autists' incapacity to play by pretending.

She quotes Leslie: 'Pretending ought to strike the cognitive psychologist as a very odd sort of ability. After all, from an evolutionary point of view, there ought to be a high premium on the *veridicality* of cognitive processes. The perceiving, thinking organism ought, as far as possible, to get things right. Yet pretense flies in the face of this fundamental principle. In pretence we deliberately distort reality. How odd then that this ability is not the sober culmination of intellectual development but instead makes its appearance playfully and precociously at the very beginning of childhood' (p. 171). Leslie lucidly speculates about this with good reason, but he thereby challenges the essential postulates of cognitivism and we will be returning to this.

Frith illustrates decoupling with the example of the film *Citizen Kane* and the newspaper headline stating that the candidate was 'found in love nest with "singer".' The inverted commas indicate here, without stating it explicitly, that this was certainly no singer! They indicate decoupling and the word therefore represents something else – a non-singer. Strangely, Frith overlooks the fact that inverted commas, which I use every time I quote her faithfully, mainly to criticise her views, primarily indicate the integration of other people's words into language, which would tend to support her argument, which goes further from the outset by pointing out that here they indicate an innuendo (sexual in this case) that signals the speaker's duplicity.

We can only agree as to the importance of communicative elements decoupled from reality in language and the pertinence of the view that autistic people seem to have difficulties in manipulating meta-representations, which confines them to a literal understanding. For once taking a moderate line, Frith considers that there are gradations in this deficiency in decoupling, which means that some children are able to attribute beliefs while remaining impervious to bluff and counter-bluff.

Frith takes Leslie's theory and his view that this relates to a late evolutionary stage of the species as confirmation that a single neurological deficiency explains Wing's triad – a deficiency in social contact, communication and playful imagination. Its late appearance in development is taken to justify her assertion that early detection is impossible and its explanation of the impediment to accessing other minds as separate then provides the key to all autistic symptoms. Frith concedes, however, that repetitions – rituals and stereotypies – and strange intellectual aptitudes cannot be explained by this alone and this has forced her to adopt a broader aetiological approach.

She quotes Milton, an intelligent autistic 12-year-old, who when asked how he has learnt something answers: 'By telepathy', (p. 175) because he is incapable of associating something he has learnt with anyone else or with anything he has read. She then returns to literal understanding with the striking example of a little girl who had been terrified when a nurse at the hospital said 'Give me your hand' (p. 178) in order to take a blood sample, having taken this request literally, thinking that her hand was about to be severed!

Are there any therapeutic benefits?

Frith is certainly forced to acknowledge that her theory does not imply any possible form of treatment, since she goes no further than recommending love and a structured environment. However, she believes she is making a major contribution by avoiding imputing maliciousness to a child whose behaviour we find puzzling if we misunderstand his handicap, which she likens to scolding a blind child for bumping into furniture. More pertinent is her advice to explain what we are saying to an autist, without assuming that the implicit context is self-explanatory by attributing our own mental states to the child, who has only a literal understanding.

More alarmingly – and this reminds me of a criticism that I will later be making of Winnicott – when Frith takes the example of Lesch-Nyhan syndrome (a combination of mental retardation, motor disturbances, self-mutilating behaviours and gout), which was found to be entirely due to an enzyme deficiency, this is to add that restoring this enzyme did nothing to cure the illness!

Frith concludes her book with a simple reassertion that her discovery of a cognitive handicap has superseded all other theories of autism. She also makes a remarkably judicious observation concerning the inversion of the causal connection between the deficient mother-child bond and autism, emphasising that it is autism that is responsible for the lack of warmth and love between them, not the other way round.

Critique of the cognitivist position

General critique

Although it represents a welcome advance on the behaviourism from which it emerged, cognitivism is still strongly confined within a somewhat naïve positivist and scientistic ideology. This is a naïvety that is not shared by the true scientists who explore the nature of reality in physics: they have had to reckon with uncertainty, unpredictability and complexity.

The cerebral organic origin of psychic malfunctioning remains a defining premise for this movement, although some modern hypotheses appear to refute this. For instance, the plasticity of the brain shows that synaptic connections are not entirely genetically programmed but undergo a process of construction, especially in the earliest years of life. With his *neural Darwinism*, Gerald Edelman[2] puts forward the hypothesis that selection occurs through the experience of certain connections, applying to the psyche the principle of his approach to immunity. The body is not programmed for every possible aggressor; it is programmed to recognise new ones. Unexpected confirmation of this view that the brain is programmed for structuring through experiences has come from the recent decoding of the human genome and the slightly vexing discovery that we have only 38,000 to 40,000 genes, while even the earthworm that is most studied by geneticists, with its 200 neurones, and the fruit fly have 20,000 genes! With only twice as much genetic material, there is no room to programme the connections of four billion neurones.

It should be noted that the infant's innate skills, well described by Brazelton, involve by definition a recognition of the part played by genetic programming in establishing early relationships. If early relationships in turn participate in the brain structuring that will organise subsequent experiences, it is necessary to conceive of a two-stage fusion in complex interactions in psychic construction. This indicates that the alternative between organic and psychic genesis is obsolete.

The other naïve positivist premise is the self-evidence of a passive and inevitable perception of the world as it is, which is thought to be an obvious given for human beings. However, we know that even our computers, implicit models of the operation of thought since Turing, are incapable of recognising something unknown. If you try to put a Mac-

---

2 *Consciousness: How Matter Becomes Imagination.* By G. M. Edelman and G. Toroni. London, Penguin, 2000.

formatted disk into a PC, it will not tell you that it does not understand this unknown language; it sees nothing and treats this foreign entity like a void. In considering how the brain processes information – which is progress compared to the simple consideration of *inputs* and *outputs*, entrances and exits, to construct a theory of the black box that processes information – cognitivism does not question the self-evidence of the existence of this information about the world and other people. What is not self-explanatory is the *cathexis* of these objects as worthy of interest, and psychoanalysts think that this cathexis is underpinned by the drives. The hallucinatory aspect of the dream shows us the active component of perception of the world in the daytime, and delusion shows us the ever-present possibility of recourse to a defensive recreation of the world. From the psychoanalytic perspective, perception is in one sense a successful hallucination. As is emphasised by the ethnologist, Jean-Marie Vidal, a *theory of love* is the prerequisite for a *theory of mind*. The artificial and unquestionably defensive splitting between intellect and affect in cognitivism places a severe constraint on its capacity to theorise psychic birth.

It should not be forgotten that when Turing designed his famous machine, the ancestor of artificial intelligence, he explicitly set out to create a machine that would reason in a way that was neither masculine nor feminine. We know that Turing committed suicide, possibly because he was persecuted for his homosexuality. This tragic outcome is a reminder that objectivisation can so easily be put in the service of the denial of human affectivity and sexuality.[3]

On autism

The scandalous claim that early detection and treatment are impossible

I think the reasons will have been clear for my alarm when, as the result of her otherwise exciting research, Frith presents us with the conclusion that both early detection and treatment of autism are impossible. These two assertions are in fact merely the consequence of her aetiological bias, which is in no sense proven. In fact, the earlier treatment is undertaken, the greater the chance of preventing or diminishing the strange situations that she herself describes so well. It has been my impression that early

3 There is a psychoanalytic critique of cognitivism in a multi-author work: *Psychanalyse, neurosciences, cognitivismes. Débats de psychanalyse*, Paris, PUF, 1996.

treatments with mothers and children (and fathers) have increased the chances of a child acceding to language. Early treatment in a day hospital, enabling the child to experience living with other people, unquestionably diminishes his incomprehension of the implicit aspects of social life. This viewpoint that early diagnosis is useful is one that is shared by others.

Under the direction of J. L. Adrien, Professor Sauvage's team in Tours has developed a scale for evaluating autistic behaviour in children (ECA-NI),[4] which enables us to distinguish between autism and retardation from 13 months of age. In this, 6 of the 33 items studied are significant: stereotypies, frustration intolerance, tantrums, intolerance of change, dislike of being touched and hugged, an exclusive interest in physical contact and finally indifference to the acoustic world. This figure rises to 19 out of 33 at the age of 18 months. This team also worked with family video recordings.

The English Checklist for Autism in Toddlers (CHAT) emphasises the importance at 18 months of age of the incapacity for play involving pretence, the absence of proto-declarative pointing and the deficiency in joint attention. We see that this scale takes account of the cognitive acquisitions that *benefit from early detection*. The 'pretending' game is highly ingenious because the child has to offer his mother a cup of tea, which enables a wish of the mother's that is unrelated to that of the child to be represented, and an identification with a third party that he finds satisfying. We can see that the drive dimension and its triangulated processing underlie this, at least in my view.

From a Lacanian perspective, Marie-Christine Laznik suggests that the installation of the drive circuit passing through the mother is lacking, as is the child's pleasurable anticipation during the games in which a child's mother tenderly plays at eating him. In my terms, this subtle observation attests to the absence of an oral masochistic phase. Freud does not dare to name it directly in his famous 1924 article on masochism,[5] formulating it as the fear of being eaten. Anyone who plays with young children knows that the role of Little Red Riding Hood is just as exciting and sought after in these games as the role of the wolf!

Theory of mind can emerge

Victor was a young boy of about seven years old at the time of the episode

---

[4] In *Devenir*, vol. 6, no. 4, 1974, pp. 71–85.

[5] The economic problem of masochism. *S.E.* 19.

that I am about to relate. His teacher[6] criticised him for doing something that endangered him and other people during a walk and formally issued him with a punishment: on his return, he would 'not get any melted cheese'. This was goat's cheese on toast, which the teacher would make on returning from the walk and that the children liked. This punishment made a strong impression on Victor and he kept repeating this sentence ... for the next six months! One year later, another seriously stupid action on another walk brought a new threat that his teacher skilfully left unformulated: 'You will be punished when you go back to the day hospital!' In the small minibus that drove the children back, Victor's voice was raised and he exclaimed: 'Punished video!' It should be explained that Victor was the only child at the day hospital who ... hated the video! He never watched it, and never asked to see it. It seems to me that a child who spontaneously suggests that he should be deprived of something that he does not like is demonstrating an excellent theory of mind and is saved for humanity.

Soliman was a good-looking child, as diabolical as Sean Barron, with malicious eyes when he was being disobedient. It had been impossible to keep him in his class because of his aggressive behaviour despite his obvious intelligence. At the day hospital, he attacked some other children, and overturned all the chairs that he found in his way for ... over a year! His communicative moments were highly endearing and he talked but it was constantly necessary to battle with his little devilish side, which was exhausting for his family and for us. When a very excited (non-autistic) child arrived, who was fairly strongly disposed to stupid behaviour and disasters, Soliman discovered that he could make him do the things for which we scolded him and delighted in seeing him reprimanded instead! This shows fine access to a theory of mind and the entirely human characteristic of duplicity. One year later, Soliman's mother approached me with a great deal of tact and delicacy: her son had told her 'Denys is sad' and she thought I might be suffering in my personal life. This had not in fact been the case, but I remembered having shouted several months earlier during a great battle with Soliman: 'I'm very sad that because of your stupid behaviour you can't go to school any more!' This was profoundly true. Soliman had thus preserved inside him this moment of emotional truth that I had expressed. Before leaving us, when he was eight years old, there was further progress in his theory of mind. A small girl with a

6 Patrick Le Hir de Fallois, a psychologist as well, who also developed a productive practice in a form of theatre group.

strong propensity for biting was causing us some concern, when I saw Soliman openly placing his forearm under her nose. A few minutes later, I saw him coming towards me, showing off a forearm adorned with a fine bite mark. He told me, with a very pained expression: 'Soliman's father will be very angry!' Getting a friend punished was already something, but getting his psychiatrist scolded by his father seemed to be a much better idea!

For anyone who is inclined to doubt this, I can easily adduce the example of Temple Grandin, when she denounced her enemies for the punitive strike that she had herself carried out in the teacher's garden: what an equally fine illustration!

Ignorance of the sexual drives and denial of suffering

Frith quotes an autist, Jay, who called the period of adolescence between 17 and 21 years of age 'the student nurses age group' (p. 125), explaining that other people might give it a different name. For example, his electronics teacher might call this age range 'the American Television Electronics School or ATES age group', since most students at that school were from the same age group as the student nurses. From this, Frith draws the conclusion that an autistic person as skilful as Jay has not understood the need for a name to be shared for the purpose of 'two-way communication' (p. 126). She nevertheless recognises in this case a capacity for thinking about other minds. On another occasion, Jay was worried about having written that a friend had a 'whiny' rather than a 'nasal' voice, whereas he remembered having said that this word – which he copied from his sister – might be hurtful (he compares it to using the word 'nigger') (p. 129). He added that he himself had had a whiny voice the year before. Frith concludes from this that the 'whiny' voice represents something more than what the young man said about it, beyond the adequacy or otherwise of his description of a sensory quality. However, she can only establish the excessive quality of this worry and the difficulty in decoding intentionality that leaves autistic people helpless when confronted with irony. This is true, but the 'more' that is meant here is abandoned in favour of deficiency and we will not find out from her why Jay attached importance to it.

Let us consider another line of enquiry. It seems to me more scientific to consider an alternative hypothesis as well. 'Whiny' denigrates the acting of whining, or expressing your sadness, as if you should not cry for so little reason or you should have got beyond the age of expressing your emotions. Here are two problematic dimensions for autists: expressing emotions and especially suffering, on the one hand, and leaving childhood, on the other – Jay thought he had been 'whiny' himself only one year earlier. Having conceded that Jay could be unhappy and susceptible to humiliation (he referred to a criticism his sister made of him), we might be able to consider attributing some sexual drives to him: it would not then be very surprising that the image of the already sexually desirable young people – the 17–21 year-olds – should be associated more with the student nurses, defined here as young girls, than with his fellow students at the electronics school, most of whom I imagine were boys. In any case, the student nurse is more of a fantasy for the apprentice electrician than for the student nurse who mixes with them. These are desirable young girls for daydreaming about, and it is noticeable that their occupation contains a caring and thus maternal vocation, which could be important for a young man who might sometimes want to cry, and who was afraid of being teased if he did, as his sister had done, undoubtedly jealous of the priority inevitably accorded to her brother by their mother on occasions because of his problems. However, here I would agree with Frith again in imagining that Jay has not necessarily understood that his sister's denigration contained some jealousy.

This example shows the author's blindness to anything that would constitute a drive dimension and the conceptual impoverishment that unfortunately ensues. This is despite the fact that she gives the platform to autistic people who express affectivity and suffering, as on page 136, where David's autobiography concludes with his despair about not having any company as he gets older, or when she cites one of Kanner's patients, Jerry, who has grown up and is describing the horror of his school years: 'Elementary school was remembered as a horrifying experience. The classroom was total confusion and he always felt he "would go to pieces" ' (p. 103).

We have also seen how Frith avoids confronting the intolerable issues of self-mutilation.

There is some plain dishonesty in the way Frith rejects the research conducted by her colleague Hobson, who recognises the role of affects and their intervention in *early* communications between mother and child. Hobson, who is a fellow experimental psychologist and is equally convinced of the innate character of disorders, poses a direct threat to the denial of affectivity and affects, and therefore suffering. Moreover, he locates the disorder and its observability at the very outset of life, destroying the entire complex edifice of the second stage that is said to be required for the deficiency in theory of mind to emerge!

The arguments adduced by Frith here are particularly weak: 'It has been taken for granted too readily that early bonding and attachment formation is missing in autistic children, and that this lack is the purest manifestation of their core symptom. The currently available evidence suggests that there are two serious problems with this belief: (1) lack of early social responsiveness is not universal in Autism and is probably rare in more able autistic children; (2) non-autistic children also lack this ability, but later are less socially impaired than autistic children' (pp. 148–149).

In her experiments on theory of mind, the fact that only some of the autistic children present the abnormality and some retarded children also have it does not prevent Frith from generalising her theory and making this an invariant! She does not explain which data 'suggest' a challenge to Hobson's well-argued and precise work. This is therefore not remotely scientific. It turns into blatant bad faith when, as we have seen, she suggests that a very early disturbance in recognition of emotions may result from a general difficulty in recognising mental states, which is precisely what she argues presupposes a much more developed level of psychic construction, a point that matters very much to her. This strange line of reasoning might be interpreted as follows: I am right because that which contradicts my view of early life is only one particular instance of what I believe in, which I think appears much later!

The rejection of a psychic defence

This rejection is a further very weak point in this theory and once again it is ideologically motivated. In fact, there is no obvious reason why an organic origin to a psychic impediment should eliminate the possibility that a psychic defence is at work, with effects that are sometimes positive and sometimes negative on this impediment.

It is the ideological opposition to the former psychogenetic hypothesis – postulating a relational deficiency in the mother as the origin of autism – that needlessly radicalises Frith's standpoint. When we discover a chromosomal abnormality that disturbs a child's psychic construction, this does not eliminate his psychic life. On the contrary, it complicates his task – with feelings of envy at successes from which he is excluded, anxiety aroused in other people and the parents' regressive temptation to regard him as younger than he is rather than as older and afflicted or restricted.

When we get a commonplace physical illness, we generally only take anti-inflammatory medication, struggling much harder against a painful surplus in our defences than against the inaccessible attacking virus. Why should the autistic psyche be considered purely in terms of a handicap without a defence at work? That is why this doctrinaire theory cannot account for self-stimulation or self-mutilation: these require the concept of a psychic defence at work through or against excitation! In short, they require a human destiny, as in each of us, with unavoidable conflicts.

However, let us move on to the more central debate about a defence in autistic retreat.

We are indebted to Jean-Marie Vidal[7] for providing evidence of an autistic defence at work through an experimental system that allows its objectivisation. Vidal organised a series of meetings between an autistic person and an experimenter, then alternated meetings with two people with meetings that introduced a third party (always the same person). The recorded analysis of the patient's gestural and verbal reactions demonstrates a change in reactions when the third party was introduced. With all due respect to Beate Hermelin, the filing cabinet has less cause for complaint than the psychiatrist, who in turn has less cause than the third party who intervenes in a dual relationship! Kanner's young patient, who was only going to use the sledge that his parents had put in the garden for him early in the morning when there were no other children playing there, would already have been able to convince of us this …

Misunderstandings

Possibly as a result of an innate cognitive disorder, our English cognitivists have clearly never heard of Winnicott's work or read his book *Playing and Reality*.[8] Less surprisingly, because this is a French author, but also regrettably, they have never taken an interest in Lacan's work on intersubjectivity in the 1960s. From Poe's *The Purloined Letter*, which describes the game of chance in which one player has to guess whether the other has an odd or even number of objects in his hand, Lacan explains how the child who has to guess has to form a hypothesis about the other's mind in order to ascertain whether he should guess the same way again, which presupposes that his adversary does not believe he is so stupid that he simply changes them over. The entire argument of Poe's work is to show Dupin considering the mind of others in order to determine the destiny of the letter whose actual content there is no need to know. Lacan goes on to accentuate the problematic with the famous example of the prisoners, one of whom will be released if he can solve a

7 J. M. Vidal, 'Dialoguer avec des autistes' [In dialogue with autistic people], *La Recherche*, 301, 1997, 36-39.

8 1971, London, Tavistock Publications/ New York, Basic Books.

riddle that includes a number painted on their backs that is only visible to the two other prisoners. Admittedly, Lacan's work then moves ever closer to the idea that the primary object participates in creating the child's psyche. Lacan's answers are debatable, but the question remains nonetheless pertinent, and this is completely eliminated from cognitivism, despite the fact that this emphasises the lack of separation between the child's mind and the other's mind.

CHAPTER 4

Clinical practice: some points of convergence between psychoanalysis and cognitivism

IT IS IN fact highly instructive to compare the cognitive and psychoanalytic approaches if we go beyond the differences in terminology, and I shall be proposing that there are some parallels in an attempt at translation that proves to be surprisingly productive.

Non-differentiation between self and other

As we have just seen, theory of mind presupposes a concept of other minds as distinct from one's own, the absence of which seems to be paradigmatic of autism. Similarly, Winnicott and Tustin regard the hypothesis that the distinction between the child and the external world is not self-evident as the starting-point of psychic life. Esther Bick, with her concept of adhesive identity, does likewise, as does Didier Anzieu with his 'skin ego' concept and Bion, with his model of the container-contained. Of course, all these hypotheses are then developed along different lines but fundamentally they share the same starting-point: challenging the self-evidence of the internal-external distinction for the psychic apparatus.

Literalness and adhesiveness

The literalness emphasised by the cognitivists can usefully be connected with the adhesiveness proposed by Meltzer. In fact, adhesive cathexis – clinging – necessarily implies a one-to-one correspondence between word-representations and thing-representations. For my part, I have suggested that this should be understood as a testimony to the defused libidinal component of the drive, an all-or-nothing cathexis that is fixed in a solidified temporality.

Lack of coherence and the life and death drives

When Frith refers to the lack of a *drive for coherence*, an absence of synthesis in autism, she also comes disconcertingly close to Freud's theory of the life and death drives, sometimes described as his metaphysical reflections. For Freud, it is the life drive that operates to construct 'ever greater unities' in the synthesis (1923, p. 258).[1] Cognitivist *fragmentation* is strongly evocative for me of the work of the death drive, which perseveres in 'breaking to pieces' that which is human to the point of a return to the inanimate state. I have argued that the death drive accounts for the *dismantling* described by Meltzer in autism, since this dislocation occurs without apparent anxiety. We know in fact how terrible psychotic fears of disintegration are. However, autistic people for once seem to be protected by the sacrifice of their being, their identity and their ego: having nothing to lose seems to be the best form of protection against annihilation. An army that disbands and goes underground becomes invincible. Meltzer does in fact use military metaphors to describe dismantling.

Once again, I should emphasise the importance of drive defusion, which alone accounts for this economic (in the drive economy sense) paradox concerning anxiety: the death drive brings about unbinding. However, although drive defusion protects from ego anxiety at the cost of this ego's very existence, it also prohibits any construction or psychic work, which can be accomplished only in a moderated combination of connection and detachment. Nothing can be built on sand and little with cement alone – sand crumbles and cement solidifies into a fragile block – whereas mortar made of both sand and cement enables the construction materials to be combined in a solid and lasting way. Similarly, the binding operated by the life drive and the unbinding that results from the death drive will, through a fusion of the two drives, enable the cathexes to be moderate, temporary, reversible and exploratory. If they become solid and are damaged by life, with great suffering a work of mourning will be possible and a renunciation will finally emerge, opening the way to a new capacity for love.

With building bricks, children are able to make temporary constructions by trial and error. Their main feature is that they can be put together and taken apart. Daniel is deprived of this, with his tower that he obtains no pleasure from breaking down. In their play, normal children try out a prototype of psychic work and precisely this prototypical function of making a draft version, modelling or approximation.

However, we should note that the cognitive model is nevertheless a positivist one. It assumes a drive for coherence and regards its absence as the onset of destruction: fragmentation. Freud's second model, which postulates a destructive drive in human beings and locates conflict within,

---

[1] Two encyclopaedia articles. *S.E.* 18.

is more scandalous. This theoretical standpoint that there is only a positive impulse also exists in psychiatry. This was the view taken by Henri Ey, who was influenced by Jackson and his *organodynamism*, with a hierarchy of mental functions that is subject to disorganisation. Some psychoanalysts, who tend to be monists rather than dualists, in philosophical terms, are not immune to this line of thinking. Pierre Marty's psychosomatic theory thus seems to be underpinned by the idea of a vital organising impulse, disorganisations of which are the consequence of failure rather than the result of a conflict.

From my own perspective as a psychoanalyst, it is nevertheless important to acknowledge a destructive impulse in the human being. Anyone who doubts this has only to open a daily newspaper or think about recent human history. This does not mean, as a naïve conception of psychoanalysis reduced to a liberation of drives would suggest, that this self-destructive impulse should be idealised or bowed to in the patient. The autistic retreat that is mutilating for the child does not have to be respected. Quite the reverse – identifying the danger and assessing its full scale helps us to confront and combat it more effectively. In psychiatry, naïvety on the part of the therapist is not something that is gifted to the patient – quite the opposite.

Cognition and knowledge of space and time

Tustin and Meltzer, as well as Winnicott in more general terms, have shown us that there is nothing self-evident about a sense of security in one's own or others' existence. However, in childhood autism, Tustin and Meltzer have identified some major differences in how the world is perceived and established that neither space nor time is acquired. Meltzer argues that space here is two-dimensional, a depthless surface, and that time is oscillating or circular rather than existing on an axis, which is reversible in psychosis under the impact of megalomania, leading to self-procreative fantasies or has an irreversible trajectory in neurosis (normality), leading to mourning and loss, but also to hope and desire. There is a clear divergence here from Leslie's assertion that these are innate. This leads psychoanalysts to conceptualise extremely severe disturbances in perception – and *knowledge* – of the world. Is this so very different from describing fundamental disturbances in *cognition*? It is therefore solely the assumed origin of this deficit – an abnormality in the active psychic construction of perception for psychoanalysts and a genetically based organic deficiency for cognitivists – on which they are divided.

The importance of play

The criticism that Frith fails even to mention Winnicott and his work on play is based of course on the acknowledgement of an encounter with this field, which gives such a valuable insight into childhood. It is even possible in the light of the cognitivist works to see – as we will do – a useful reassessment of the play dimension in the institutional treatment of autism. If the incapacity to play is an essential feature of the pathology, it follows that play is a vital aspect of treating it!

The 'meta' dimension

In her emphasis on the importance of meta-representations and their absence in autism, Frith unwittingly concurs with an entire field of psychoanalytic research on symbolisation in the normal or pathological psychic apparatus. For my part, I have observed how autistic children take more interest in boxes than their contents, and emphasised how a child playing with water was setting up a situation in which a container contained not only some contents but another container. She was twirling figures around in the felt-tip pen case, which was itself contained in the toy box. Water was being poured from one container into another, as in many kinds of water play in our fountains. This container of a container simultaneously led into the third, with the space around the contained container being left free for something other than itself in the container surrounding it. This space shows that there is no adhesion as there is between the layers of an onion. Hannah Arendt uses this metaphor to describe the totalitarian social system in which the adhesive dimension seems to me to be crucial.

The idea of introjection of the containing function is central in Bion's concept of the *container-contained*, in which the psychic work carried out by the mother (or the analyst) enables the child first to assimilate his emotional experiences, metabolised by the parental intermediary, and then to appropriate this capacity for metabolisation itself.

Developments in psychoanalysis

There have been major developments in psychoanalysis in the last few decades, with a move away from the underlying ideology in Bettelheim and Winnicott, along with the idealisation of the mother's role in early life. Although Bettelheim states in his theory that the mother is not responsible for her child's autism, we have seen that his countertransference is much more negative. In his 1966 paper on autism presented to the Society for Autistic Children, Winnicott states that he agrees with Bettelheim[2], and he acknowledged their suffering as greater than the child's. However, he cannot disown his view, and is so convinced of the immense importance of the environment in early psychic construction that he can only confirm the harmful nature of deficiencies at this time. In consolation (!), he reminds them that doctors have also made mistakes with the very best of intentions and gives the terrifying example of thalidomide, which caused children to be born with deformed limbs! However, in another article, a lecture given in Paris, he explains his views on maternal unconscious aggression and murderous wishes. For him, these are harmful primarily in terms of the loss of all spontaneity in the mothers, in the throes of the inhibition of their drive impulses, both positive and negative. He does not seem to believe in an omnipotent maternal unconscious but is convinced as to the tragedy of the loss of spontaneity in contact with the child.

We must therefore acknowledge that parents are right to protest at the oppositional stance adopted towards them by psychoanalysts in the 1950s.

The point that I would like to make is that this is not an indictment of too much psychoanalysis but, rather, reveals an insufficiency. In fact, Freud advanced psychoanalysis by questioning his theory of traumatic seduction in the sexual domain in order to recognise the role of fantasy and deferred action in patients' allegations of seduction by adults. Why did we accept as historical fact the guilt-induced version that parents elaborated in order to protect themselves from a meaninglessness that is intolerable to the psyche, which cannot dispense with causality and prefers guilt to helplessness? It is sometimes, in a grotesque way, a collapse without medical consequences that the parents reproach themselves for not having been able to prevent and to which they attribute the cause of the child's psychic disturbances. It is much more often their love or their audacity in wanting to have a child that they feel is at fault when confronted with his arrested psychic development.

It is therefore more psychoanalysis that is required to help them, recognising the form of defensive psychic work involved in the parents' elaboration of the child's history.

By accentuating the importance of the primary object in psychic construction – and the acquisition of language through the mother tongue

---

[2] Autism. In *Thinking About Children* (pp. 197–217), ed. R. Shepherd et al. London: Karnac, 1996.

shows the relevance of the question – Lacanian theory runs the risk of privileging the psyche of the parent who is suffering and talking while sometimes forgetting that it is the child rather than the parent who is our patient. However, some analysts using Lacanian theory today fully recognise how organic or genetic afflictions can restrict the psychic development of some patients, without in any way abandoning their psychotherapeutic ambition towards autists, as stated by Marie-Claire Camena d'Almeida and Sylvie Lapuyade.[3]

The valuable psychoanalytic standpoint of respecting the patient's material without influencing it presupposes a psychic apparatus that is capable of integrating a therapeutic setting and of being aware of the respect that is being shown to him. In the course of her work, Tustin manifestly develops her approach to moments of autistic lifelessness and thereby combats them more actively. She makes a comparison with drug addicts and says that with them, as a drug addict told her one day: 'Parents have to be stern in their love' (1986, p. 293).[4] The stereotypies are therefore then energetically combated by seeking to bring the child back into contact. Meltzer gives the clinically valuable indication that the dismantled child has to be sought at the level of skin contact. He considers in any case that there is a 'loss of maturational mental lifetime which is replaced by autistic states proper' (1975, p. 16).[5] This view simultaneously fully recognises the handicap that is constituted on a daily basis and encourages an active approach to bringing the child out of it.

Our naïvety has been to apply to a patient who has to find access to the other and to his own desires through psychotherapy an ethical code that is only justified when both these have already been acquired at the outset. It is rather as if I only accepted for analysis patients who were capable of love that was genuinely free of any narcissistic component and fully recognised otherness without any fetishistic element in their sexuality, as well as being secure in their identity and bisexuality and aware of their conflicts of love and hatred... This would raise the question as to why they would need to come and see me!

In institutions influenced by psychoanalysis, we have been criticised

---

[3] Psychanalyse et autisme. Quelques aspects sociohistoriques et cliniques [Psychoanalysis and autism. Some sociohistorical and clinical aspects]. *Les Cahiers de l'actif*, no. 280/281, La Grande Motte, Actif Information, 1999.

[4] Tustin, F. *Autistic Barriers in Neurotic Patients*. London: Karnac, 1986.

[5] Meltzer, D. et al. *Explorations in Autism: A Psycho-Analytical Study*. Perthshire: Clunie Press, 1975.

for not assisting the child in danger and the issue arose from respecting the child's distance and waiting for him to become able to express a request and a wish for stimulating activities before involving him in them. This question thus cannot be so easily dismissed. It was not from a lack of interest or capability that Fernand Deligny patiently and rigorously followed the child's wanderings, mapping out his 'meanderings' to keep track of them and try to fathom their meaning. However, for me it has yet to be established that this wandering has any other meaning than a sign of dismantling or indeed that it has any meaning at all.

Furthermore, the strategy of a firm and attentive but non-intrusive presence produces results in anorexia, which is known to be potentially fatal. Many young autistic people are in fact anorexic. By dint of seeing us eating fairly happily with their young friends, they often end up stealing bread between meals or pinching food from someone else's plate, and then escape from the terrorising vicious circle – and here the word is justified – in which they confine their parents who fear (with reason) for their lives.

However, here again we should acknowledge that the paradoxical quality of anorexia is a mode of relationship and that an autistic person who avoids contact has not necessarily achieved this.

It seems important to draw a distinction between the period of the session and the remainder of the treatment during the day, as is possible in a day hospital setting, whereas a child therapist working alone confronts this problematic only during the session. This institutional care does not involve one vast day-long session, as some might have wished. Although during the session we will later discuss what is to be done with the repetition – Daniel's crayons and building bricks – this leaves other times in the day available for requiring his presence during group activities, alternating with other informal periods that preserve the possibility of the unexpected emerging.

Let us reconsider the neurotic patient in analysis. I ask him to give free rein to his emotions and his associations during the session by abandoning active control of his psychic life during that time. However, for him to be able to pay me and to construct his existence, it is absolutely necessary for him to manage his finances properly and therefore take on the constraints of active work the rest of the time! Every action is forbidden him during the session, so that anything can be said. However, I hope that he has a private life and a body living out its sexuality and power at other times of day and night.

Just as a child in psychotherapy continues to attend school, why should the autistic child be deprived of teaching, education and socialisation on the basis that he is in analysis? This would mean we were staking an infantile and omnipotent claim to be everything to him, like the mother of a baby. This would merit being analysed as a matter of urgency!

Psychoanalysts, who are required to have carried out extensive work on their own areas of madness and illusion, should therefore be expected to accept a degree of helplessness and the sharing of positive contributions towards a child, while acknowledging that he may be physically ill and require medical attention. Would this castration of omnipotence be so intolerable? We will see that although the answer seems obvious, the heated reactions on all sides testify that when confronted with childhood autism and its tragedy, parents and professionals often find themselves resorting to primitive mechanisms of psychic survival.

Developments in cognitivism

Cognitivists have a cultural advantage over psychoanalysts: they consider themselves to be scientific and have therefore been elevated in a culture in which the refutation of a theory testifies to its scientific nature, as Karl Popper emphasises, and it is therefore easy for them to accept theoretical developments (provided of course that they come from within their own ranks!). This has had the beneficial effect of bringing the intangible nature of this lack in theory of mind under challenge.

We have seen that Hobson has argued for the importance of affect in understanding other people and it can only be cause for rejoicing to see affectivity thus reintroduced into the relationship. For Colwyn Trevarthen, this lies in the importance of the infant's early exchanges with his mother, who uses a primordial *motherese* that is demonstrated in his theory of a primary disturbance in the emotional regulation of cognitive development. In the context of a theory of an innate lack of equipment, he restores to early relations their place and importance in psychic construction. If early exchanges are acknowledged, affect is rehabilitated and the psyche can evolve, it will be easier to engage in productive discussions!

I sometimes catch myself imagining my work being read by a cognitivist and I then feel like proposing to him some research topics, such as pain and negativity.

Pain

The assessment of pain is a theme that is fortunately fashionable in paediatrics. Some pioneers have reminded us that the child's physical pain was long neglected. Thus, children were not even offered analgesics for diseases that were nevertheless acknowledged to be extremely painful in adults, requiring morphine treatment. The notion that the child's nervous system was immature protected the caregivers and doctors from atrocious imaginings concerning that which they were having to inflict. Thus thoracotomies were performed on newborn babies without anaesthetics!

In addition to the denial on the part of therapists for very simple psychological reasons, a characteristic of the child's acute pain is that it manifests itself by retreat rather than calling out or crying. Thus, when morphine treatments were continuously injected through a portable pump to children with cancer who were lying demoralised and apathetic in their beds, they were soon found playing in the playroom on the same floor.

I would therefore point out to my cognitivist reader that thinking that the severest psychic pain forms a part of autistic retreat is not a stupid supposition. Despite still not having dared to treat autistic anxieties with major analgesics, I would be very interested if researchers were to apply their skills to evaluating pain and anxiety in autism.

Negativity

Some years ago, there was a fashion among manufacturers of felt-tip pens for including an eraser pen in the felt-tip pen cases that I was using in my materials in sessions. This greatly amused the neurotic children, who would draw in the negative with the eraser pen having produced a background or rub out a sentence that they had written as if it had to undergo repression. It seemed to me that the psychotic children were generally not very interested in this capacity for negative writing, as if that dimension were inaccessible to them.

In our mental work, the capacity for erasure is absolutely essential. How can we concentrate unless we shut out all the intrusive stimuli? The extraordinary memory that autistic people display may simply demonstrate the lack of a capacity for forgetting, an adhesive perception of reality. Do we need to remember every detail of our daily journeys, of every advertisement or text we have ever read? Every sentence uttered by other people or ourselves?

In a classroom, a blackboard or whiteboard has the advantage that it can be erased for the next class. If you imagine that every sentence written had been engraved in marble, how many lessons could you give a pupil before he got lost in a vast mausoleum?

When we read a book, we manage to see nothing but the line we are deciphering and this alone, negatively hallucinating everything around it. Our train of thought itself presupposes the elimination of the previous thought and many of the perceptions of external, and especially internal, excitations. The repression postulated by Freud therefore forms the basis for secondary-stage thought, protected from unconscious primary processes and affective and emotional disturbances.

Autists' extreme sensitivity to sensory perceptions and their extraordinary memory may be connected with a lack of negative capacity for erasure or negative hallucination. Like a draughtsman without an eraser and clean paper, how can they work without the right to make an error, without a free space, without forgetting anything? André Green developed a concept of the work of the negative[6] in the psychic apparatus, which emphasises its absolute necessity and productiveness there. Now this is an exciting field of research! Provided that they moved away from a positivist ideology, experimental psychologists would undoubtedly have a great deal to teach us if they were to venture into this almost certainly crucial domain.

How can we generalise, seek out that which is similar rather than identical, unless we are able to erase certain differences, a very human kind of work in contrast to the computer operations that brilliantly reveal the exact nature of the resemblance. We have all been exasperated at some time by an over-precise machine that, for example, does not find an author in a search because his initial is followed by a full stop or because an accent is wrong. This is why the recognition of writing, language or a face is a challenge for the computer scientist, whereas it is self-evident for the human being, who is lamentably handicapped, however, when it comes to precisely memorising data. Alas, the 'Rain-Man' type of feats in autistic people are entirely mechanical: the hero of the film memorised the telephone directory, but of what conceivable use is that to him? Just imagine having nothing but these printed pages of a telephone directory as writing paper!

It is concerning these capacities for transformation and learning that we need new information and creative research. In such a context, should we not be pursuing some new lines of enquiry?

---

6 *The Work of the Negative*. London: Free Association Books, 1999.

CHAPTER 5

Re-evaluating institutional therapies: some questions arising from facilitated communication

DURING THE PERIOD when there was a vogue for the TEACCH method, confusing schooling with behavioural re-education, many parents were strongly attracted to the serious and useful aspects of the method, and we strove to explain to them why we considered it more important for children to learn to live together, to play and joke around. Psychoanalytic institutions thus gave the impression of being lazy and disorganised, as well as reprehensibly casual. Just think about it: so-called professionals were playing with children, wasting public money!

This French educational tradition represented a form of practical knowledge that was difficult to theorise for specialist educators and professionals concerned with the onset of psychic life. By indicating the inability to play and to pretend as a crucial symptom of autism, Uta Frith renders us the great service of demonstrating the importance of the capacity for pretence and play in the autistic problematic. When I played wolf with some young children, drawing on my medical thesis that academic pressures prevented me from entitling 'Tra-la-la, the wolf!', I gained a sense of the importance of small groups for stimulating children in their psychic and cognitive development.

'The three little pigs' is a masterpiece of suspense, repeating the threat of being eaten three times in a temporal mode that is progredient in its repetition. There is the threat of being eaten, but also the wish to eat and, less easy to admit, the wish to be eaten. We were familiar with the importance of working on the child's drives by putting them into cultural forms – stories. Knowledge of these is normally heartily devoured.

Placing the emphasis on the capacity to play has the advantage of going beyond the contents to address the symbolising matrix. By playing in a day hospital with other children, the autistic person is working on the vital issue of communication with others and his belonging to his age group, and his socialisation progresses. However, he is doing more than this: he is tackling a tragic element in his pathology and experience shows that, albeit very slowly, his capacities increase and are enriched.

Back to Winnicott: the capacity for play

We are indebted to Winnicott for his reassessment of the importance of play in the psychic construction of human beings. He must have shocked more than a few psychoanalysts by arguing against the received notion of child psychoanalysis as an adapted form of adult psychoanalysis, in which play substituted for the adult patient's language and associations because of inadequate capacities. Not only did he regard play as an essential part of every psychoanalytic treatment; he reversed the proposition to state that play was universal and psychoanalysis was a particular form of play! He set out to demonstrate how the analyst has to bring out the capacity for play in the treatment of some borderline adult patients. Play is in fact for him one of the child's primordial activities, which contains all his later creativity in embryonic form and is indispensable for an authentic sense of existence. Taking the paradox further still with the famous aphorism of the 'created-found', Winnicott makes the child's creative capacities the precondition for his discovery of reality and therefore his subsequent access to objectivity. This constitutes an indisputable contribution by psychoanalysis to the understanding of the meta-communications that give access to culture.

Winnicott worked a great deal on the importance in psychic construction of an intermediate – *transitional* – space in which an illusion is shared. This subsequently opens the way for the child to the space of creativity, art and culture. The self-evidence of the sharing of implicit references to a common cultural reality originates here. This involves for the child a space in which he does not have to decide whether he has found or created this object, whether it is internal or external. This gives a sense of how necessary such spaces are for human beings to recognise their essential similarities (let us think for example of religious beliefs and their foundational roles in human societies) and how these seem to be tragically lacking in autism.

'Represented' witnesses:[1] *facilitated communication*

Several years ago, a technique originating from Australia had a major impact on many parents of autistic children: *facilitated communication*. It was developed for cerebral palsy sufferers in order to try to restore

[1] This is the term applied to witnesses who are facing charges themselves, which I have adopted for its emphasis on the questions surrounding the veracity of these testimonies and its connection with the rights of defence.

some of their individual capabilities by enabling them to express simple choices about their daily lives. It was possible for instance to ask the patient what he wanted for pudding by offering him two pictures to choose between and starting to move his hand towards the pictures. Despite being incapable of speaking and instigating this movement, he was nevertheless able to control the direction of his hand and move it towards the picture that represented his choice. This felicitously postulates a psychic capacity that is superior to the patient's spontaneous instrumental operativity and certainly helps to give him some dignity as an individual. The technique was amplified with pictures of the alphabet that made it possible to understand some words, followed by simple typewriters with which it was possible to produce words on a strip of paper. The film *Johnny Got his Gun* (1971) provides a good illustration of this issue of misunderstanding a human being who is imprisoned in his neurological handicap. Recently, a man who suffered a major vascular attack managed to write a book[2] before he died by batting his eyelid to indicate which letter he was choosing.

The application of this principle to autism has given rise to the dream of the intact child who is immured in silence by his physiological inability to communicate. This method has proved remarkably effective among parents opposed to psychiatry as a result of its neurological premises. Many parents who had abandoned any hope of being able to talk with their child and had adopted the defectological ideology of the TEACCH method were thus paradoxically confronted with the hope of a miracle that had only been deeply buried. With autists, the 'facilitator' starts moving the child's hand and holds it until it reaches the keyboard, which obviously raises the question of how to determine who is writing. In terms of establishing its scientific objectivity, the results are damning. When the keyboard is hidden from the child, it works anyway, and when the keyboard is hidden from the facilitator, it stops working! The same applies if an observer stands in for the facilitator. Nevertheless, some astonishing testimonies have emerged, as we will see, and, furthermore, when after a long period the facilitator is merely holding the patient's elbow or shoulder, it becomes difficult to dismiss the technique entirely as a piece of mystification. It is already clear that physical contact seems to be necessary for maintaining it, which appears to make sense in terms of an adhesive identity that is maintaining a psychic unity, as with a mother and her child.

---

2 Jean-Dominique Bauby, *The Diving-Bell and the Butterfly*. Translated by Jeremy Leggatt. London, Fourth Estate, 1998.

It is therefore in terms of an anticipatory illusion that I understand the therapeutic effect of this method before the patient is able to provide any evidence that his production is autonomous. Just as a mother who talks as if her child understands her fosters the onset of what she anticipates, the facilitator who co-creates a text that expresses the patient's affects, perceived and felt by dint of hysterical capacities, gives the patient the sense that what he is feeling can be put into words. A psychoanalyst does exactly the same thing when he draws on his perception of his countertransference. However, this presupposes that the psychoanalyst has undergone a personal analysis in order to avoid unwittingly projecting his own problematic on to the patient. Hysterical suggestion can just as easily work in the opposite way for the facilitator and lead her to attribute her own feelings to the patient. Inadvertently kindling the patient-therapist chimera (de M'Uzan), facilitated communication is then confronted with the problematic of hysteria: suggestion and seduction. In a lecture in Paris, Jane Remington-Gurney issued a warning to her audience, explaining that some Americans had found themselves in prison following the production of some texts accusing them of sexual seduction!

The fundamental problem is that this type of relationship involves a belief on the part of the facilitator in order to create a favourable illusion but entails all the risks of belief. This is what I explained in my preface to the book by Anne-Marguerite Vexiau,[3] who developed this technique in France. My colleagues, whom I had encouraged to explore this avenue, did not wish to pursue the training, having been put off by an atmosphere of excessive belief. Some parents complained to me about value judgements on their private lives – for example, a divorce – that were attributed to their child in the texts. Another mother felt that she was being manipulated by the texts produced, which fiercely attacked her. The stereotyped quality of the texts does in fact give rise to the fear that they say more about the facilitator than the child. 'In the day hospital they think it is my head that is ill when it is my hand' may be an expression of Mme Vexiau's beliefs rather than those of my patients. There are also some disturbing mystical assertions, when young Israelis 'write' in French about Mme Vexiau's God 'which is love' (pp. 283–290), this is slightly perplexing.

However, it would be unfortunate to reject this approach entirely because of some possible misapplications. It is providing some encouragement and a fresh perspective to parents who are seeking to understand a child whom

---

[3] *Je choisis ta main pour parler* [I'm taking your hand to speak]. Paris, Robert Laffont, 1996 (translated quotation).

they had despaired of being able to reach. One parent testified that a text addressed to the child's grandfather made reference to something entirely unknown to the facilitator. It seems to me that it would be possible to try out a demythologised and demystified approach by accepting the joint creation of these productions and temporarily setting aside the question of their authorship. There are in fact some grounds for hoping that the facilitator's ego is being put in the service of the child's psychic apparatus in order to express uncontrolled psychic productions like an auxiliary ego, fostering the child's appropriation of these skills. This amounts to giving full consideration to a psychotherapeutic role – something of which A.M. Vexiau seems to be aware today – but which would therefore justify a personal training in consequence.

The productions of the facilitator-child pairs are highly narcissistic – which seems to fit with the autistic problematic – and demonstrate a strong transference on to the facilitator – who often receives a marriage proposal – which is also not surprising, unless it proceeds from a secret romanticism on the part of the adult. The parents seem in any case to testify that the children are putting a lot into these sessions that they have organised outside our therapy, and we respect this.

Birger Sellin: an imprisoned soul [4]

Birger Sellin is a young German autist with no language and violent stereotypies, who appeared in a television documentary. He types his texts with his mother. As a young child, he used to leaf through books belonging to his intellectual parents in an apparently sterile stereotypy. He had amassed a marble collection, and his parents were astounded one day to hear the sound of his voice, when his father had casually picked up one of his marbles. As he left the room, he heard him say: 'Give me that ball back!' (p. 12). His parents then reconsidered their impression that their child was unreachable and went to see a practitioner of facilitated communication, whose role was then taken over by Birger's mother. The texts produced are so strange and what they relate is so unexpected that if they had been created by this mother, she would be a great poet indeed. However, even if she had been inspired, it is impossible to understand how she would have arrived at these melancholic themes of unworthiness. This is not the way a mother would fantasise about her ill son.

---

[4] *I Don't Want to be Inside Me Any More: Messages from an Autistic Mind.* By Birger Sellin. Translated by Anthea Bell. New York, Basic Books, 1995.

It should immediately be pointed out that Birger Sellin is suffering from secondary autism – he could speak when he was two years old and had thus internalised language before the regression he experienced after being sent to nursery school, where he constantly screamed, which was followed by an infectious illness. Furthermore, this context is highly specific: a diagnosis of post-encephalitic retardation is said to have been suggested after a period in a psychiatric hospital that was originally meant to last six weeks and was finally extended to six months! It is therefore equally plausible that this child's disorder emerged only at a secondary stage, coinciding with a psychic ordeal (being sent to nursery school), an infectious illness, the detrimental effects of a period in hospital that cut him off from his family for six months when he was two years old and all three of these factors in just about any combination!

Birger therefore writes with his mother. The publication of the original texts convincingly demonstrates his preliminary attempts at some hesitant words and unpredictable letters, until the appearance of a first sentence addressed to his mother: 'i love you' (p. 41). He writes that he has known how to read from a very early age and in several languages. He explains that while leafing through the books, he was recording and memorising entire pages at a glance, then reading them calmly at his leisure. 'i have read many extraordinarily impressive books since my fifth year of life and i hoard all their important contents in me like precious treasures' (p. 198).

This extraordinary capacity for instant memorisation is commonly reported in autists: as with the telephone directories in the film *Rain Man*. This is also reminiscent of the English autist who managed to draw an entire Victorian building without making a mistake about the number of window-panes, having seen it for only a few seconds. This is a total and immediate adhesive perception that we have to accept is possible. It should not be cause for wonderful speculation because it draws on a primitive functioning that Jean-Pol Tassin, the neurophysiologist, relates to subcortical brain functioning. In the psychic apparatus, rapidity is the opposite of elaboration, which uses extenuated pathways and inhibitions in order to accomplish genuine psychic work, as Michel Neyraut emphasised in relation to traumatic neurosis.

Writing is not easy, however, for Birger: at first, he only manages to write five to ten lines in an evening. This is what he says about facilitated communication: 'i so often get the letters wrong without help but when someone is holding on properly it all goes easily this is like a desolate image the fact is even a word can be very eventful it can stir you right up'

(p. 75). He wants to learn to write alone, worrying that everyone will think that his mother is producing what he is writing. He manages to write a little with his father and makes a subtle observation by commenting that it was difficult to do this on one particular day because his father was sad about the mother being ill. This finely illustrates a theory of other minds and a recognition of the third person loved by the other, unless this is his own emotional state being projectively attributed to his father, which again would be an achievement for an autist.

Birger went through an entire developmental process that we will leave the reader to discover from his book. At certain times, he is hardly writing any longer; at others, however, there is in fact a personality transformation that results from the possibility of exchange. He expresses his love for his family, his parents and his brother Jonas, who is ten years younger, but he also protests and poses questions. Thus, he writes to his mother: 'an exceptional mother mustnt be angry with a lonely steely person' (p. 108) and 'are you sorry you ever brought confused idiotic totally crazy birger into this important world' (p. 120).

His style is so strange that it produces the conviction that we are hearing something that has never been said before, a thought constructed in the most desperate depths of solitude, with the extreme narcissistic tonality of megalomania or in the abyss of self-denigration. I shall reproduce the absence of punctuation and capital letters in these quotations: 'ive often been scared because people didnt know i could understand everything so they just said everything things i wasnt meant to be hearing ... i would like to suggest everyone is extra sensitive because i can hear a bit too much and see a bit too much but my sense organs are okay its just that im afraid theres a muddle going on inside words sentences ideas get all torn apart and the simplest things get wrenched out of the way they connect up in the important real one and only other outside world a thought is really difficult like being boxed up in the inside world' (p. 23). This is a dismantled or fragmented thought, whichever term is preferred. Let us explore its main themes.

The depths of despair

Birger expresses a melancholia – in the psychiatric sense – with a very deep sense of unworthiness: 'a power forces me to keep quiet about it its like a demon forcing me such a monster it keeps making me repeat things all the time to hiss do kidstuff and lead a crazy persons life its like an eternal battle ... people like birger make them frightened and have to be isolated a bunch of crazy folk' (pp. 106–107). One year later, he writes:

'i receive crazy orders sour as vinegar from the heart of the strange festering command center responsible' (p. 203).

In addition to an unexpected sense of guilt, Birger strikingly expresses the emergence into non-existence by something that seems to me akin to what Meltzer terms *dismantling*: a 'non-ego': 'looking for totally stupid firm tricks so as to punish someone like steely totally eager birger he punishes himself it is just stupid to give up the security of this house anytime i can be so safe withoutme any time that i am peaceful but that peace means being dead...' (p. 114).

For him, only we 'creatures steely in their freedom of speech' (p. 97) can have access to language – and he is totally excluded from this. He does not consider himself 'worth being able to talk' (p. 86) but is deeply sad at being misunderstood, apart from slightly by his teacher, 'and the others dont take any trouble with a person like me any more its enough to drive one to despair' (p. 78). He realises that his grandfather has died and expresses his sorrow, while regretting that he cannot cry 'properly to weep out an unspeakable huge lonely wedge inside me weep out a whole existence would be the only personal comfort' (p. 88).

Anxiety

Should anyone still be in any doubt that autistic people suffer, he need only pay heed to Birger's text that dates the anxiety back to his return from the children's psychiatric hospital to which he was sent: 'then i was afraid of everything' (p. 106); 'do you really know how deep-rooted anxiety can be in an individual / the way it eats away an individual / the way it works personally on a single person at the collapse of the first agonizing words' (p. 80).

'one anxiety i suffer from most of all is how to survive a day / from the settled viewpoint of a chosen person that must surely seem ridiculous / i for my part / protect against the icy times of day / by setting up a socalled iron important list of questions / an idiot system as it were running away from anxiety ... (p. 118).

Like the other autistic people whose testimonies we have heard, he describes a fear of falling: 'calm is certainly very superficial a state worth aiming for but an important condition isnt that simple first there is the anxiety coming on in bucketfuls' (p. 121).

Birger also reports hallucinations: 'once i went rigid with fear unintentionally because i thought dripping waterdrops were living creatures / it was only when i looked more closely i saw they were waterdrops / sometimes i still get illusions like that but they dont scare me as much as they used to' (p. 94).

In correspondence with his mother's psychology lecturer, Gisela Ulmann, he writes – and to my mind he might equally well have sent a copy to Uta Frith:

'it is nonsense making simple mental problems out of important questions the way gisela does she is working on the theory that anxiety is a flaw in the mind but anxiety is something which cant be grasped so easily it is a disturbance i am afraid it is so strong that i cant describe it my autistic behavior gives an impression of it for instance screaming and biting and all the other senseless things' (p. 117).

The progress comes at the cost of a heightened anxiety – 'so much anxiety that the earth can hardly bear it' (p. 154) – that can no longer be assuaged by stereotypies, testifying perhaps to the painful reinforcement of the ego, which might explain the regressions that are so trying for those around autists:

'an old simple way of seeing things / a going out of oneself / a crate from which i am rising / that would be a dream such as everyone dreams / but i dont see any way out of this crate which is me / even this important writing isnt enough / a way out destroys my old security' (p. 116).

How instructive this is for anyone who does not believe a defence is at work in autism! But how equally instructive it is for anyone who is combating the psychically mutilating but terribly efficacious defences and is thus confronted with the violence of their stringency as they require the child to exist and thus to feel, to suffer this denied pain ... through self-denial.

Autism

'i could only talk the way i write if the autism was gone and that wont work because there isnt any cure / it is a disturbance which cant ever be properly described / its cutting off a person from his first simple experiences like essential important experiences / for instance weeping / just weeping without feeling angry beforehand and / laughing the way children laugh' (p. 86).

Stereotypies

'rustling [running his marbles through his fingers] is stereotypical behavior which is really intoxicating i am only doing visibly what loneliness does invisibly' (p. 109). Birger explains that it is also a defence that can be substituted by knowledge: 'knowledge steers clear of socalled repetitive actions first attempts to keep from being delivered up to chaos' (p. 105).

Teachers and crises

Birger explains that he had a temper tantrum at the institution where he is being treated because he was: 'irritated by important teachers / an example of how they annoy me is that they just talk on / and on in front of me as if i was air / i seize the first socalled opportunity to interrupt them and / i scream bloody murder / how that happened today i dont know myself' (p. 98).

This must give some pause for thought as to the cause of the incidents previously described by Asperger, which must happen more often than we realise! Birger goes on to state: 'we often call on repetitive behavior instinctively safely just immensely / we are really bent on amusing people / by rousing them from peace to an attack of rage / being nice without thinking about it calls for powerful control of this instinctive difficult behavior' (p. 123).

Birger Sellin does not have the disarming lack of malice that some people attribute to autistic people and he can be an acerbic critic. He describes his institution as 'a really crazy what you might call madhouse of the lonely class / i am sure important amazingly vain people arent good for much anyway / but those tremendously vain beasts of mixedup teachers certainly arent' (p. 124) and he writes about interrupting them with his screaming.

The teaching offered to Birger had been gradually simplified, as he did not seem to be 'getting it' and it is one of the great lessons from this testimony that this phrase, either heard or used about an autist, should ring an alarm bell. Accordingly, at his institution he is taught that potatoes grow in the ground, which is modest in ambition, but true. In writing, Birger communicates that he would like to know how language expresses feelings, and he later wants to attend (accompanied by a teacher) some university lectures on Renaissance love poetry!

Desires

Birger Sellin longs to go to a disco and he remembers that he had his first ejaculation while listening to a Michael Jackson record, which he has very much liked ever since! It is a 'strong song sung fast in haste' (p. 67) about the world being destroyed by bombs. However, he also expresses a desire for knowledge, 'a burning hunger for knowledge from understanding ... a passionate desire / to be one with people who know / to be one with the ordinary people who lead lives without any confusion / just like a valuable essential respected other person like a person with dignity' (p. 115). He no longer wants to be 'inside' himself and says he has been 'afraid of the end of the road and the end of humanity' (p. 72). Finally, in the Gulf war, he would like ... to go and kill Saddam Hussein!

Time and the gaze

Birger makes some observations about time. He clings to the rhythm of light and darkness – 'the clock of the lonely is a visible socalled system of lightdarkness' (p. 99) and says that his concentration is much better in the evenings. There is an enigmatic text about time: 'like everything else a date happens to be a matter of rotating events / its a fact time serves the purpose of a little of the total eternal centrifugal onedimensional / framework in which we humans live' (p. 80). He goes on to consider the temporal abnormality as the cause of his autism:

'i cannot organize time like socalled normal people / i take my bearings from banal things like just mealtimes and times for going to bed and getting up / i cannot look for torn time / it is eternally extinguished from a realm engendering time and cannot be brought back / by torn time i mean the time at a persons disposal / and which pitilessly restlessly fills up my idiotic insanity in bucketfuls within eternally unique uncertain uncertainties / i dont know any words in our language to describe this terrible phenomenon / is this important inexplicable crazy phenomenon the cause of my madness...' (p. 196).

Birger writes that his visual perception is too acute, like his hearing stricken by sounds, but that 'inside me i can simply switch it off / and within seconds / all i see is a high wall of dots' (p. 139). This is reminiscent of Donna Williams' account, but may also result from a radical decathexis of perception. In contrast to Frith's descriptions of the inability to understand the exchanging of looks, Birger directs a criticism at his mother:

'a single word said in love can heal any number of wounds / and a loving look does wonders without words / i think even the look in the eyes is part of a persons character / you are often lovingly eager to see rough words / but your eyes look bad / only little jonas is really always kind' (p. 123).

Development

Birger is about to receive a visit from a film crew who are planning to make a film about him. He admits that he has to hide from everyone so that he cannot be seen trembling with fear. He thinks 'its nonsense asking god to help me / a god who makes autistics cant keep on punishing such horrible people' (p. 155). He would like to reply to the letters he receives, like Donna Williams, and he wanted to write to her, but did not dare to do so. He criticises the film *Rain Man*: 'a film like rainman cheers you up / but it doesnt show any of the total chaos the vast anxiety and incredible sorrow and loneliness / in us this film shows a facade for purposes of entertainment' (p. 182). He manages to exchange letters with some other autistic people who are using facilitated communication. The level of exchange and elaboration increases until some more metaphysical questions are posed in the final texts: I am selecting an extract that I find striking because it seems (to me) to illustrate my sense of an advanced drive defusion between the life and death drives in autists.

'there is one thing thats crazy / being in yourself is a dead state / being without yourself is loneliness / neither being in yourself nor without yourself can survive / there are no pure states / there is always change taking place in me / and even in calm times two forces that wont be reconciled are working' (p. 222).

Again, we will allow anyone who wishes to accompany the author further on his journey to read Birger's book, which he concludes with the following address to the reader: 'i wish you a simple but internally whole and very loving life your dark nonperson birger' (p. 225).

Katja Rohde

Also German, Katja Rohde is the author of *Ich Igel-Kind*, which she translated into French herself.[5] Again like Birger Sellin, she expresses herself little verbally, and it is not until she is 23 years old that her encounter with a speech therapist who uses facilitated communication reveals through this medium an intelligence preserved in the young girl, who had been considered to be severely mentally handicapped by the various institutions that she had attended.

Following a difficult birth and postnatal resuscitation, she had to stay in hospital for two months before being returned to her parents and once again we find circumstances that support organic damage and trauma in the establishment of early relationships. To this must be added

[5] *Ich Igel-Kind: Botschaften aus einer autistischen Welt* [Hedgehog-child: messages from my autistic world]. Munich: Nymphenburger, 1999. *L'Enfant hérisson*, Paris, Imago, 1999 (page numbers here refer to the French edition, from which the quotations are translated).

an original circumstance: while her mother was pregnant with Katja, these parents started looking after a little girl whom they then adopted, which meant that her adoptive sister, who was one year older, had only been in the household for five months when their mother had to leave the child when she came to give birth. This separation while another child needed looking after cannot have made for easy relations between Katja and her mother.

Troubled by her child's apathy despite the paediatrician's reassurances, Ulla Rohde initially obtained diagnoses of mental retardation, then a diagnosis of autism, which she felt was a better explanation of what she felt her daughter was experiencing. However, the book and the mother's concluding testimony mainly describe the unsuccessful struggle to obtain recognition of this characteristic in institutions for handicapped children. In contrast to the situation in France, where parents of autistic children reject psychiatry and call for the recognition of handicapped status, this mother has struggled against a status of mental deficiency for her daughter. In accordance, however, with demands currently being made by these parents' associations, the book makes a plea for integration into normal schooling and arrangements that would allow Katja's particular intelligence to benefit from being fostered.

Incapable of dressing herself or wiping her bottom, Katja was only able to attend school because her parents were teachers, and at first this was just for two minutes a day in her mother's class, accompanied by another teacher. In addition to that, her stereotypies and noises were beginning to annoy the children who had accepted this experiment. However, the two minutes gradually became two hours, followed by access to some other subjects, but she suffered greatly from not being able to follow the same course as the others afterwards.

Katja and her mother feel extremely bitter towards the institutions for failing to recognise the young girl's capacities or to acknowledge their mistake after she started producing some texts, one of which was read out at the institution's annual party without attracting a single comment from these professionals. However, this is a criticism that Ulla Rohde and her husband also direct at themselves. Some fleeting signs might have alerted them to their daughter's capacities, of which they had been completely unaware. This is one of the disturbing elements of these testimonies and in my own experience, because many strange moments of wondering if something has happened in a dream are experienced by caregivers and reported by parents.

When Katja had her first – very heavy – period in the restaurant of a motorway service station during a journey, her mother, having been overtaken by the events in the cramped toilets, exclaimed on returning to the table: 'I don't think it's fair that a big baby has to have periods!' The family then heard Katja clearly state: 'I am not a baby'. Another time, when her mother was teaching her how to identify some car journeys on a new itinerary and asked her where she had to go, Katja said a word very like 'hospital' that had appeared on one of the signs. Finally, her mother remembered hearing Katja reply 'no' in German when a waitress offered her some cheese in French during a journey in France, which was where they usually went on holiday.

Katja's texts provide the explanation: from the age of four or five years old, she had been taking books from the family sitting-room to read them alone, hiding to do this, and with an unmistakably 'photographic memory'. She learnt the Latin dictionary and secretly benefited from what her sister Pamela had been learning in this subject for school. She learnt and wrote French as well because of the family holidays in France ... and because her parents spoke French when they wanted to talk about the children without being understood by them! She knew some basic English, Italian, Arabic, Russian and even a little Swahili because her mother had made preparations for a trip to Tanzania with Pamela.

The texts, which are much more fluent than Birger Sellin's writings, are characterised by an astonishing auto-didactic pedantry, combining Latin references and Biblical quotations (Katja often called herself Esau) with frequent religious allusions (she is the hedgehog, God's creature), elements of Nordic mythology and the attribution of an exemplary value to the 'defeat of Sedan' in the war of 1870, in fact a French defeat – but Katja was extremely Francophile. Accordingly, every setback is a 'defeat of Sedan'. Once again, and in a different way, this strangeness gives a fairly convincing sense of the authenticity of this testimony obtained through facilitated communication. To this is added the fact that several facilitators were able to help Katja.

Her testimony shows a tender-hearted pity towards her mother and scant tenderness towards herself, and she is harsh on the teachers in the institutions for the mentally handicapped.

'As I grew up, without making any progress, I annoyed my mother: I screamed at the top of my voice, I peed in my pants, I raised my hedgehog prickles as soon as she caressed me, thus creating illusions about my state of mind when I wanted to be recognised. I left my mother feeling hopeless, as she fussed over me; she had apple cheeks, she was agile-minded and atheist. I left her with no hope. She was convinced that God's creature was the malformed creature of Jesus and that I was not made to succeed through divine will. I destroyed my dear mummy's hope, I destroyed it fundamentally' (pp. 34–35). 'My father didn't help either: he saw my autistic behaviour, he didn't understand it' (p. 35).

Katja describes her suffering:

'No one realised that my screaming at the top of my voice, my autistic behaviour, was in reality an intense protest at my anxiety attacks, dead, sad, sad, sad unto death, dying, of anguished and loud cries ... A dark despair like a terrible shore made me scream, me, the hedgehog child' (p. 28).

She was humiliated at being in a school for the mentally handicapped (and remembers her teachers secretly making fun of her mother for believing that she was autistic) and expresses this in an original way:

'The conduct resembling that of Mireille Mathieu, or Elisabeth of Austria, which was that of the teachers, dealt a blow to Esau's desire to learn from them ... As the child whom God had wanted to create, and who needed love, I with my hedgehog ways annoyed these teachers, who had no help and who tried to calm me down, and I made them exclaim: 'What a little imbecile! What are we going to do with her'?' (p. 29).

She then criticises the affective coldness and 'the outmoded ideas about autism or the total lack of any idea on the part of the staff', finally commenting that although they respected the people who were capable of imposing these on them, her mother was defenceless before 'their mixture of self-importance and arrogance'.

This is a further hard lesson, for what specialist can be certain of never having abused his powers? How can we avoid allowing parents to nurture the illusion that would give them the wrong idea about their child's real nature without risking enacting, like the teachers on this occasion, a rejection of the intolerable despair at the child and the parents' suffering? We should also remember that Katja's mother did not believe the speech therapist either at first, and that the father then refused to believe his wife!

It should next be pointed out that like Sean Barron, Katja seems to cling to her mother's hope. Furthermore, the subtle and highly convincing observations concerning the varying attitudes of professionals towards the person opposite them demonstrate a perfect theory of mind! Similarly, she remembers that one teacher lied to her mother, who was worried about the state of her teeth, and gave her masses of sweets.

Again it can be observed, as with Birger Sellin, that the narcissistic dimension, with its flaws and its compensations, features strongly in this testimony and that Katja demands the same fate as everyone else without being able to accept her limitations. She cannot overcome her impediments, even though she is suffering from her toilet-training problem, which drastically reduces her autonomy.

Unlike Birger Sellin, Katja is very clear about her erotic desires: she wants a man and is in love with the conscientious objector who accompanies her in the class, but she has understood that he only felt liking for her and loved someone else. Her appeals to other boys remained unsuccessful and she refused to enter into a relationship with some autistic boys to whom her mother has introduced her: she wanted a normal lover! She was also worried about being alone and childless for ever.

Before accepting him, she had been very jealous of her young nephew – apparently of mixed race – which suggests that Pamela is a girl of African origin. Is this why Katja often quotes *Othello*, in which the Moor embodies jealousy? She in fact only speaks fondly of Pamela, who has always supported her and guided her towards the world. This would mean that she has access to the repression of her jealousy, which would be a neurotic capacity.

The book ends by raising a rather grim question, although these testimonies – still suspected of mystification – are the stuff of dreams for every parent and caregiver of autistic children without language. What other possible solution is there than being in her family for an autist who reveals such a discrepancy between her very limited capacities for social autonomy and her intellectual abilities, which cannot be expressed without the combined physical and psychic support of an emotionally cathected facilitator?

Discussion

Even when we are aware of the blind spots and beliefs that can be engendered by parents' despair, however much they guard against the risk of financial exploitation through speech therapy sessions in facilitated communication and the associated risk of a benefit being derived consciously or otherwise from the belief in its magic, such testimonies cannot be dismissed out of hand. Their originality and their unprecedented quality in unique styles that nevertheless resemble certain characteristics of testimonies from autistic people who are capable of expressing themselves alone, make a convincing argument for us to take them into consideration.

These two testimonies have the common feature of noisy autistic symptomatology in autistic people without language. Elements of organic affliction are possible or probable. However, with due respect to Katja Rohde, I do not at all exclude the possibility of a combination of a deficiency and autism. It might be wondered whether these two cases do not in fact accord with the neurological hypotheses of facilitated communication, in which case they would not be generalisable. However, both children have shown this mnemic capacity that is absolutely characteristic of autism, and both describe an intense anxiety and an endless despair.

However, it does not follow that every subject who presents autistic symptoms has the same secret capacities. What conclusions can be drawn from this? Since there is no way of knowing, we must work from the basis of our uncertainty. We must envisage the possibility that capacities that the subject is incapable of assuming with reference to others may in fact be present, at least as a potentiality. How is this to be ascertained? It would be desirable to have a reliable expertise in order not to overlook valuable hidden characteristics.

This certainly makes me question my misgivings about an autistic child attending school without having any real chance of following the teaching, for I did not like the idea of a child being accorded the charitable status of a 'learning disability'. If we accept that a child can take in more than he appears to do, then this has another meaning in terms of exploring a potentiality for dignity, as when we talk to a child without knowing whether he can understand us, in order for this to happen. On reflection, it is certain that if we were only allowed to attend a concert if we could play an instrument we – in my case at least – would not often attend one. This does not mean that we are incapable of detecting a wrong note, regardless of whether we know any music theory.

With young children, it seems to me that the therapeutic work should tackle the essence of autism, the non-communication, retreat and mutism, before seeking out original lateral pathways of communication. This makes me reticent about aids to communication based on pictograms or sign language because access to language is an indispensable element of communication. After the age of ten years, however, it seems to me that every possible avenue should be explored in seeking a psychic life.

This does not prevent us, in my day hospital for young children, from having two Macs in the classroom for children who find that the typing process or the machine itself disinhibit their access to reading and writing. Finally, I would reiterate that I see no conflict between treatment and education, and that both are necessary, wherever possible in a genuine integration that is then conducted on a part-time basis. There again, the situation in nursery schools is much more flexible, and I recognise that the task is more difficult in primary schools, in which absence from some of the classes disrupts the rhythm of learning.

CHAPTER 6

Scientific discoveries and the implications for body and mind

Biological research

INFLUENCING THE PSYCHIC apparatus does not require a denial of the body, and biological research is fully compatible with a biological approach that at present – regrettably! – has yet to provide any treatment, but which there is every reason to pursue. It is possible to take into account both the psychic *and* the biological aspects. Accordingly, Dr Sylvie Tordjman set up a research study that combined some biological tests with a chart for data collection, developed with Geneviève Haag.[1]

I recently encountered an example of the misdiagnosis of a case of subacute epilepsy despite exhaustive medical examinations in a child who presented an uncertain and variable clinical profile of confusional autism. The child's mental activity was undoubtedly affected, as a basic electro-encephalogram would have detected. A pioneering cortisone treatment for one year improved his brain functioning, but at the cost of a year of hell for the child, the parents and ourselves. He had become irritable without his discomfort having been reduced in any way. Today, however, progress has resumed, and some fragments of language with a communicative function have emerged.

The avenue of endorphins

There has been some investigation of the hypothesis that the offspring of opiate-addicted mothers presented stereotypies at birth in some experiments conducted on animals. Autistic people often have higher levels of endorphins – those natural forms of morphine – in their blood platelets. However, Sylvie Tordjman observes that this amount is more an indication of stress and does not give information about the levels in the brain, which for ethical reasons it is not possible to discover. This model resulted in autists being offered a treatment with naltrexone, a morphine antagonist, and

1 *Psychiatrie de l'Enfant* [Child psychiatry] Paris, PUF. 1995, no. 2, p. 38.

one of the children from my hospital has been included in such a research procedure at his parents' request. It has had some mildly beneficial effects according to the experimenters, but the placebo has produced the same results. The parents' hope and the discipline imposed on the child as he undertook the treatment may account for this.

New points of convergence: pain

We can observe here that conflicting methods have led to a point of convergence in the field of pain – for biologists, an excess of internal painkillers and, for psychiatrists, an excess of internal pain – and the defences mobilised against these. The work of Claude Smadja and Gérard Szwec, psychosomaticians at the Institute of Psychosomatics in Paris, who developed an idea of Michel Fain's concerning the quest for calm through fatal procedures, has led to the proposed concept of self-calming procedures in the ego, obtained for example through repetitive and intense sporting activities.[2] We know that marathon-runners trigger an increase in endorphin production in their bodies. It is therefore reasonable to suppose that stereotypies and certain forms of self-mutilation might have this function, simultaneously protecting against psychic pain, treated as physical pain.

The false dawn of secretin

One day, an autistic child was taken into hospital so that his digestive functions could be tested by the perfusion of secretin, a digestion-regulating hormone. On leaving hospital, his contact with other people was transformed and his parents ascribed this improvement to the secretin, which raised great hopes for other parents who had observed digestive disorders in their children. It is true that confusional autists sometimes have such accelerated bowel movements that ingested food appears intact in their stools. Others, by contrast, seem so constipated that they can appear to be toilet-trained when they are holding back in order to defaecate in their own home. I understand these disorders as demonstrating the non-psychisation of sphincter control, which emerges at the same time as language in normal children. Inadequate or excessive control would thus emerge in autistic children in consequence of their autism. Some have wanted to regard this as a cause but, unfortunately, some American studies conducted in a

---

2 Gérard Szwec, *Les galériens volontaires* [Willing galley slaves] Paris, PUF, 1998.

sufficient number of autists have shown that secretin perfusions did not bring about any improvement in patients.

The rapid dissemination on the internet of findings from uncontrolled experiments thus regularly fuels parental hopes that are only dashed later. Some caution is therefore required before trying out the latest miracle cure or believing in a conclusive biological explanation of autism.

Developments in genetics

Modern geneticists have become very modest. They think that there is a genetic predisposition to autism that involves several genes.[3] They are most insistent that children presenting a genetic anomaly be treated by child psychiatrists and a fruitful collaboration has been established. Asperger's conviction has turned out to be correct for some patients, but with some variability in the clinical condition for the same genetic anomaly, which restores a degree of autonomy to individual destiny in relation to the inevitability of chromosomes. However, it seems to me that there is an ethical responsibility to test for a chromosomal anomaly in a child with retarded development because we must not deprive a family of critical information that concerns it. In fact, for the moment, no aetiologically based treatment is available to children suffering from one of these disorders. However, this information needs to be made available to parents in the event that a therapeutic solution is discovered. The hope must be that the rapid advances in genetics will bring us some good news in the decades to come. For parents who are going to care for their child throughout their lives, this is important.

It is important to realise that the recently discovered abnormalities are sought by specific investigative techniques, and that a normal karyotype conducted ten years ago does not exclude the possibility of a specific anomaly being discovered by new diagnostic procedures in molecular biology.[4] However, for families, the discovery of a transmissible anomaly – not the case with all anomalies – opens the way to genetic counselling for the parents as well as relatives who may be affected. It is not for us to deprive them of this through our personal convictions as to the value

---

3 According to a study recently published in the *American Journal of Human Genetics* in September 2001 (*Le Monde*, 25 August 2001), the sites of chromosomes 2 and 7, and to a lesser extent 16 and 17, are implicated in autism.

4 I should like to thank Dr Delphine Héron, who receives our patients in consultation at La Pitié-Salpêtrière, and Professor Arnold Munnich in Necker, who works on collaboration between geneticists and child psychiatrists.

or otherwise of knowing that a child is affected by an organic constraint on his psychic development. Some therapists do in fact fear that labelling a child's pathology will lead to an abandonment of hope in his prospects of changing and developing. When a second child is born suffering from the same genetic disorder in one family, it becomes entirely obvious that knowing this risk would have given the parents the possibility of prenatal screening, leaving them the choice of terminating or continuing this pregnancy. I remember a family in which the parents were told by Françoise Dolto that they were worrying too much about their eldest son and that they should 'make him go riding', which was not wrong but nevertheless deeply inadequate: he was extremely autistic! In fact, he was carrying a fragile X chromosome and his young brother was also very disturbed, albeit in a different way.

Today, some parents ask geneticists not to tell them the diagnosis for fear that their child will be refused treatment in child psychiatric services! Regrettably, there is a foundation for this because some services that claim to provide only psychic care still refuse to treat children with organic diseases. This used to be the view taken by Frances Tustin, but she added that in private practice she did not want to be conning parents if there was an obvious constraint on improvements. This viewpoint was debatable in the 1950s but it strikes me as scandalous today when many children will prove to carry chromosomal anomalies, especially in a context in which treatment costs are borne by health insurance to which every citizen is entitled. This principally reveals under-analysed castration anxieties, whereas our personal analyses should in fact have prepared us for confronting the limits of our omnipotence!

It seems clear to me that any child who is experiencing difficulty in constructing a psychic apparatus, whatever biological impediments are complicating his task, stands to benefit from intensive psychic treatment, which is the only form currently possible.

Fragile X chromosome

This is a common cause of psychic disorders and it is present in 8% of autistic cases. This particular genetic anomaly is carried by the X chromosome. The long arm of the X chromosome splits into Xq27.3.[5] Since women have two X chromosomes, if their normal X chromosome is

---

[5] P. Saugier-Veber, Les retards mentaux d'origine génétique [Genetically based mental retardation], *Psychiatrie, sciences humaines, neurosciences*, I, no. 2, 2003.

activated they become healthy carriers of the anomaly. In other cases, there are disturbances in language acquisition, which is delayed in 40-60% of cases. Half of their boys will be affected if they inherit the abnormal X chromosome, since a boy has only one X chromosome. This abnormality in the X chromosome and some others in the same chromosome, as yet unknown, are probably responsible for the higher incidence of childhood psychic disorders in boys than girls, which is confirmed by every study. To the surprise of doctors in my generation, it has been found that the increase in nucleotides (a repeat in the trinucleotide CGG, localised in the first exon of the FMR1 gene) that are responsible for the anomaly intensifies with the reproductions in the next generation. It is therefore possible for a mother to have inherited from her father – perhaps a slightly strange and taciturn character – this anomaly that will prove much more detrimental to her own children. When it is expressed clinically, this mutation is almost invariably transmitted rather than appearing for the first time, demonstrating the need for genetic screening in families.

Fragile X chromosome generally causes mental retardation and some physical anomalies that do not appear in childhood (longer lower maxillae, enlarged testicles). The children I have known with a fragile X chromosome have all had great difficulty controlling their excitation. They often bite their hands, or beat their arms like a bird beating its wings, but this sign is neither constant nor specific. Genetic investigation often finds cases of mental retardation in the patient's uncles.

Other syndromes associated with genetic abnormalities

Prader-Willi syndrome

It seems possible that one of Asperger's cases may have been suffering from this syndrome, for Hellmuth has a combination of two symptoms that suggest this: bulimia and ligamentary hyperlaxity. This bulimia poses a problem at the next stage of these patients' lives in the form of a threat to their health in adulthood from the consequences of obesity. Failing to recognise the genetic quality of hyperphagia invariably impedes the understanding of the tragedy that is represented by this uncontrollable urgent hunger. This is combined with a stubborn and obsessional character and frequent temper tantrums.

Velo-cardio-palatine syndrome (Di-George or Catch 22 syndrome)

Often combining (inconstant) cardiac anomalies and anomalies of the palate and the velum, these syndromes often cause disturbances in elocution. According to Arnold Munnich, every child who presents developmental delay with difficulties in phonation – rhinolalia ('speaking through the nose) – in connection with pharyngeal malformations should be tested for this anomaly. It is associated with a genetic anomaly (a micro-deletion inherited in 22q11).

Rett's syndrome

This is a syndrome that occurs only in girls, who experience neurological disturbances in their upper limbs, with a stereotypy that consists in rubbing their hands in a washing motion. Precise and delicate hand gestures are impossible. There is frequent hyperventilation, which can produce syncopes – terrifying – but not dangerous. The gaze is direct and non-avoidant. Around the age of three years, the symptomatology resembles that of autism. From treating one of these young patients, it became clear to me that, by establishing non-verbal communication, the psychic work with a psychotherapist and the daytime hospitalisation had transformed the development previously described as an irreversible deterioration.

Although we found her syncopes traumatic, the assurance from a cardiologist that these were reversible made us more stoical. From this day, the hyperventilations ceased, but this very pretty little girl would repeatedly fall against the edge of the table at mealtimes, with her lips swelling up and her face becoming disfigured: she had thus restored a relationship in which we constantly feared for her. She thus demonstrated a drive economy that was both masochistic and sadistic, which probably brought about the fusion of her drives and preserved her psychic life … at the cost of our anxiety!

The mutation in the gene MECP2, localised in xq28, is usually a new mutation, which therefore rules out an increased risk for other births in the family or relatives.

Angelman syndrome

This syndrome is also accompanied by a severe developmental retardation, with ataxia and groundless laughter in response to stimuli. Epilepsy is present and hyperactivity (with beating forearms) and instability are also found. Since the anomaly responsible for Rett's syndrome has been discovered, some children who were thought to have been suffering from

Angelman syndrome have turned out to be carriers of the Rett mutation. This illustrates that there is no fixed causal connection between chromosomal anomaly and the individual clinical situation.

Smith-Magenis syndrome

This syndrome is also characterised by hyperactivity, with intense temper tantrums, self-directed aggression, sleep disturbances and stereotypies.[6]

How to conduct screening for genetic anomalies

Communicating the discovery of a chromosomal anomaly is never a simple matter. Far from invalidating the psychic work, it imposes a new and highly demanding set of tasks on the parents. Their sense of guilt is not eliminated but displaced, especially if one of them is designated as the carrier. A mother thus bitterly recalls the acerbic remark made by her mother-in-law, who advised her son against the marriage when she saw the bride's afflicted brother: 'Don't marry that girl; there's a defect in the family!'

Another mother, who had also had two children who carried the fragile X chromosome, had made a connection in her psyche between her first son who suffered from this and her father, with his strange and solitary character, who had taken a particular interest in this grandson who was born shortly before he died. The night that the mother was told of her father's death, the child, less than one year old, had woken up screaming, as if he had felt his pain. This had left a deep impression on the mother's psyche, establishing a particular link between this son and her own father, who were then bound in a perfectly ordinary oedipal guilt; in the wake of her child's disturbances, however, she had felt this to be causal. The genetic diagnosis thus came simultaneously to confirm this connection – her own mother having turned out to be unharmed, it was therefore her father who had transmitted this genetic pathology to her – therefore giving the grandfather a more important part in this child's destiny than the father, and transforming its meaning at the same time. In one sense, she can be said to have felt a psychic bond between her son and her father and very logically to have integrated this in oedipal guilt, which exerts a universal magnetic force in making sense of situations. However, what did the confirmation of a link, this time a biological one, mean to her at an unconscious level?

---

[6] P. Saugier-Veber, *ibid.*

This mother had realised that one of her daughters, born before any of this information had been available, was also afflicted, from touching her skin, which was as soft as her ill brother's skin. 'A normal child has a soft skin like cotton; a fragile X chromosome child has skin like silk...' I am quoting her comment here.

Knowing about a genetic anomaly does nothing to assuage the parents' guilt: having chosen to produce a child, they feel responsible for having made love and given birth to a child who has a disease. Our task is to help them to elaborate the adjustments required of them by this accident of fate, which will remain forever engraved in the psychic elaboration of their own destiny. How is it possible for our psyche simply to integrate the meaninglessness of the chance that presides over our birth and death? Everything that relates to our procreative capacities breaks down the operativity of the primal scene as a generator of life and is necessarily traumatic.

However, for all that it should not be believed that fathers desert the scene: in fact, it is a father who is militating today in an association for parents of fragile X chromosome children and he identifies with his son. He and his wife are awaiting the birth of another child whom they have been assured by prenatal diagnosis is unaffected. However, what suffering would have ensued from having to terminate the pregnancy of an afflicted child! Alternatively, in the opposite scenario, how would we have been able to support the parents' choice to keep an ill child?

One of the things that it seems to me is most difficult to cope with in X chromosome illnesses concerns the elder sisters of the boys affected. They have a 50% chance of transmitting the anomaly. When should they be told that they too will have to wonder whether they are carrying the disease and, if so, that they may one day be faced with a choice between an abortion and having an ill child? I tend to think that what is concealed is more pathogenic than what is openly stated, which would certainly require answering their questions. However, if no question is posed, what right does anyone have to rob them of their carefree childhood innocence? On the other hand, are they in fact carefree? Are they protecting their parents by asking no questions about it? At what point then should they be told about this risk for their descendants?

It is therefore no longer possible to separate body and mind, which does not surprise me as a psychoanalyst, for Freud always regarded the constitution as a major determinant. Moreover, and in a more modern sense, Freud describes the rootedness of the psyche in the body in his definition of the drive as a demand for work imposed on the psyche as a result of its link with the body. Why would this not apply to an autist? We have seen how modern knowledge has demonstrated the subtle interaction between innate programming and relational experiences in the constitution of a human being. Autistic people are likely to be confronted with a much more difficult task than other human beings, who have managed to accede to a secure sense of existence.

I find myself wondering if certain characteristics of autistic existence are connected with a variety of determinants, some of which relate to genetic inheritance or the prenatal environment while others relate to unfortunate configurations, as we have seen for Birger Sellin and Katia Rohde, but also for Daniel, combining with life events and damaging separations, which would mean that there are several aetiologies of childhood autism. Sometimes, and more often, I end up thinking that the autistic *syndrome* is a solution for psychic survival that arises in different situations. There are neurological impediments that account for autistic behaviour in certain children affected by encephalopathy and difficulties in sensory and psychic integration, as the cognitivists suggest (but irrespective of their origin), as well as severe deficiencies of the kind that it has still been possible to find recently, for example in the Romanian orphanages. There are also unfortunate accidents of inheritance of innate relational capacities, or the equally unfortunate accident of family psychic traumas that make a father or mother unavailable at a difficult time. Accordingly, autism is a psychic structuring that occurs in conditions of access to psychic life that are extreme or deficient for a variety of reasons.

This theory has very burdensome implications: it means that many children stand to benefit from psychic treatment, which would increase their chances of acceding to communication with other people.

Autism: illness or handicap?

Of course, it then becomes absurd to preserve a polemic based on aetiology. This is not necessary for us to recognise a severe psychic illness, irrespective of how great a role has been played in its onset by organic factors, and thus the justification for intensive treatments given the urgency and the stakes involved in returning to human exchange – or to recognise its severely disabling character, which is cause for social solidarity. Eccles[7] reminds us that the emergence of human civilisation is dated, on the one hand, from traces of funerary rites but also from times when remains

[7] J. C. Eccles, *The Evolution of the Brain: Creation of the Self*, London, Routledge, 1989.

reveal that an adult member of a human group, physically incapacitated, owed his survival solely to the solidarity of the other members of this group. From this viewpoint, the solidarity of which we are capable is a measure of our degree of civilisation.

Wood's classification of handicaps

It is to Philip Wood that we are indebted for defining handicaps according to three distinct broad categories. This theory has been adopted by the World Health Organization in its international classification. These categories unambiguously differentiate the (organic or psychic) causes and their consequences:

Impairment is defined by the World Health Organization as 'any loss or abnormality of psychological, physiological or anatomical structure or function'.[8] Impairment corresponds to the lesional aspect of the handicap. It can be a temporary or a permanent condition. This does not necessarily imply that the individual is considered to be ill. It matters little whether the impairment relates to an organ or a function, and this bypasses distinction between organic and psychic aetiology.

Disability is defined as 'any restriction or lack (resulting from an impairment) of ability to perform an activity in the manner or within the range considered normal for a human being'. Disability corresponds to the functional aspect of the handicap. It increases with technical equipment or assistance. A communicative disability can be caused by a linguistic impairment.

Handicap is 'a disadvantage for a given individual, resulting from an impairment or disability, that limits or prevents the fulfilment of a role that is normal (depending on age, sex, and social and cultural factors) for that individual'. Handicap corresponds to the situational aspect of the disability. The handicaps include:

- situations of physical dependency, such as assisted independence (through equipment);
- situations of economic dependency, such as precarious independence (requiring external financial support);
- situations of social non-integration, such as relational difficulties, or social isolation.

---

[8] WHO, 1980, International Classification of Impairments, Disabilities and Handicaps (ICIDH).

An example is provided of a physical illness: a motor impairment in the lower limbs, causing a locomotive disability, will result in restricted mobility, possibly reduced physical independence (requiring another person) even, according to the severity, a handicap that affects social integration or economic independence.

Fortunately, this new classification applies equally well to autism. By moving away from aetiology and distinguishing it from the consequences of illnesses while separating the restrictions and their social impact, this classification clarifies the discussion in a way that is highly beneficial to people suffering from restricted physical or psychic capacities.

I cannot express the same enthusiasm for the international classification of mental illnesses, directly inspired by American psychiatry and its DSM-IV,[9] which is symptom-based and purportedly non-theoretical. In fact, it reflects and promotes an ideology that bases the view of the patient on his symptoms to the detriment of a consideration of his subjectivity and his suffering, an ideology that is rejected by French psychiatrists.

Children, parents and caregivers: their suffering

This process of comparing clinical experiences, indisputable testimonies from former autistic patients, controversial testimonies obtained by facilitated communication and different theoretical viewpoints clearly suggests that the suffering is indeed extreme. The autism that protects the subject from this suffering – not at all well – also exposes him to the risk of being misunderstood and this is something that should always be borne in mind.

The child's suffering

We have seen that deep anxieties are indeed always present and that projective capacities that have developed progrediently may therefore play a part in the imprisonment of the child, for whom the world thus becomes terrifying. Of the psychic agony of non-being, experienced as disintegration through precipitation anxieties, the endless fall remains present. We have also discovered some formidably intense depression, including as with Birger Sellin in people who appeared to be protected by a profound handicap from an excessively painful consciousness.

[9] *Diagnostic and Statistical Manual of Mental Disorders*, 4th edition, Washington DC, American Psychiatric Association, 2000.

Progress is therefore threatening, bringing exposure to feeling a suffering that was previously treated as such an extreme pain that refuge could be sought from it in non-being.

The need for sameness is certainly a defence against a serious danger and this remains a daily experience in clinical practice, as the following series of events shows: one morning, when I was greeting the children and their parents, there were some heart-rending cries in the distance. Gradually, these seemed to be getting closer, until I guessed that the source of this clamour was one of the children arriving: a little girl, usually delightfully amiable and very reserved, then came in, her face contorted with fear, followed by her father, who was deathly pale. The whole scene immediately evoked a drama that had just taken place. I asked him: 'What has happened?' He then explained to me the reason for his daughter's desperation. The terminus on the metro line that runs to the day hospital is at the station Nation, and they changed trains there every morning. A train had been waiting on one of the two platforms, with doors open, lit and stationary, and the little girl settled in there happily. Unfortunately, this was not the train intended for departure and it had been necessary to make her get out to wait for another train on the other side of the platform. The immutable ritual had been shattered and all her control along with it. If we recall the passion that autistic people feel for public transport routes, we can more easily understand the interest in the disintegration aroused here when both the predictability and the total control over the organisation of the daily journey failed.

The parents' suffering

We can also imagine what the child's father must be going through on the two-stop journey to Bel-Air in the view of passengers who can only be wondering what he might have inflicted on his daughter to put her into such a state of suffering.

Despite sometimes being so hard on parents, Winnicott observed that they seemed to suffer more than the children did. For twenty years, parents of the children with whom I have been concerned have taught me about the tragedy that is represented by the failure of psychic life to blossom in the child whom they have created in love. They attest to their often-total isolation when confronted with the various professionals. In the monthly meetings that they have agreed to attend, in which they can share their experiences, I have discovered how their own families sometimes abandon them or alternatively reinforce their isolation through an overwhelming concern, acting in a compensatory way towards the child, as if the parents had not known how to give what was needed. Society also abandons the parents by leaving them in charge of the most difficult situations when their child is suffering from both a handicap and fatal processes. Confronted with the injustice of fate and the absence of any response, including of course a technical one, to the question 'Why is this happening to me?', they cannot help at a psychic level holding a grudge against someone – but against whom?

There is society, which does not want to know about their tragedy, or therapists who do not perform the miracles that are always rightly expected. We have seen a protest emerging from militant associations of parents in revolt and lawsuits – as the 'Perruche' ruling demonstrates – that recognise that the child is being damaged through being alive, which poses a fundamental ethical problem for our societies. Then, of course, they can always blame themselves, since turning aggression against the self is a universal human tendency that provides some protection, albeit in a terrible way, from the powerlessness or the radical meaninglessness. Psychoanalysts should certainly not have shared this defensive organisation, less still reinforced it. However, anyone who believes it can be eliminated by rational explanation is also being naïve. The parents need above all to be accompanied by people who are not afraid of their suffering. Then they are already slightly less alone.

However, their child grows up. We must hand over to other colleagues – when we can find any who agree to do this – at the cost of participating in denial of the passage of time and depriving of treatment young children who need us and have just as much right to early care. 'I am not a baby', as Katja Rohde says. It must be recognised that a child grows up, which exposes him to being confronted with his retardation and his handicap, whereas an eternal baby would keep all his potentialities intact, but at the cost of stopping time and life. However, when, for these best of reasons, we prepare to leave a child, to decathect from him, we also abandon his parents, who have experienced great moments of trust in the team to which they have brought their suffering and who then feel dispossessed, with a sense of having been cast aside. As parents, by definition, they cannot shift the burden on to anyone else – I hope that too many demands are not made on brothers and sisters, and this is one of the issues at stake in provision of adequate social care – the burden of the vital assistance that their child needs.

However, the parents know that they will not always be there and this is something that they dread. Learning how to lead a worthwhile life in society, with or without the ability to talk, or becoming a productive citizen, is a major achievement: this will enable the parents to conclude that their child will not experience a life of terror when that time comes, if he is capable of living with other people.

A recent tragedy in which an autistic child was drowned by his mother unfortunately points to another outcome, showing that it is possible to bear a grudge that extends to murder against the child who is repudiating your love and your parental identity. It seems preferable to acknowledge an entirely understandable feeling in a story of disappointed love, including with a child, accompanied by a firm statement that the act is forbidden, than for society to abrogate responsibility through a false understanding that leaves the parent alone with the burden of his remorse. It should also be emphasised that this type of tragedy occurs when no help has been found.

Finally, the fantasy of *altruistic suicide* always seems to me to be an underlying theme in these cases. Psychiatrists use this paradoxical term to describe the situation of a parent who puts his child and himself to death. This brings a triumph of mortal fusion over psychic differentiation and separation, which is a way out of the terror about what will become of the child after the parents have died. However, the death drive has then truly won out over individuation and over life.

The caregivers' suffering

By accepting the risk of taking on some of what parents are experiencing, without protecting themselves too much from their raw suffering, and becoming involved in an emotional relationship of their own with the child, which exposes them as well to some children's desperate efforts to destroy their hope and stifle their love, as Sean Barron and Katja Rohde attest, child psychiatric workers expose themselves to being undermined at their deepest personal level. Society nevertheless does not remunerate them any better than teachers who have the pleasure of seeing their pupils (not all alas) avidly absorb the knowledge that is offered to them. We see today teachers, as well, having to deal with a different form of destructiveness that society does not know how to handle. Of course, I am including specialist teachers among the caregivers here.

In psychiatry, dealing with destructiveness is the essential task, and this is especially tragic when it makes itself felt in a child's emerging psychic life. Although child psychiatry protects from the chronic nature and desperate repetition of certain adult mental illnesses, the mortal component is certainly present and the hope invested in the development of every child admitted to the day hospital entails the risk of an endless despair. Society also fails to recognise the level of personal involvement in their work, or that many have undergone personal analyses that have helped them to elaborate their deep counter-attitudes. They are exposed to depression and this can affect an entire team. It is also possible that we have not chosen these occupations by chance and that a personal sensitivity to suffering has contributed to this choice. This is also true. It is in fact fortunate that a great sensitivity should be offered to children, but necessary that a sufficient solidity should not undermine the trust that the child is testing out. Otherwise, there is a risk of a reversal of therapeutic roles, leading to the *confusion of tongues* described by Ferenczi.

Like parents, we can also defend ourselves through universal psychic means, particularly projection and persecution. Parents and professionals can thus feel persecuted by each other and at times of conflict the depression of either group is set aside. However, the child is as well. We can also feel persecuted by the director (I have this role), the administration, the supervisory authorities (the regional hospitals agency deciding, for example, that there are too many hospitals in Paris and reducing the funding made available so that some will have to close, has very kindly occupied this role for me in recent years). Fundamentally, however, it is very healthy that we should have to be accountable to another person, which reminds us that the children do not belong to us – for dual fusion threatens us as well as parents. It is the least we can do to provide the example of symbolic gratitude from an authority, when we are asking the parents and the child to open themselves up to relationships with outsiders.

Teams can also find the way out of divisions and conflicts (which Bion defined as group functioning in *attack or flight*), and it seems to me that there is a satisfaction of the death drive taking place when intractable splittings lead to schisms or expulsions of scapegoats. In contrast to Paul-Claude Racamier, who considers that it is sometimes necessary to encourage toxic members of a group to leave it, I therefore feel it is always beneficial to seek to understand these types of conflict as something that drains and gives an outlet to the destructiveness of psychotic and autistic patients. However, conflicts and departures are also part of life, and an institution set in stone would be equally pathological. There are healthy departures to participate in other adventures, which is something I learnt from Francine Klein, the psychiatrist and psychoanalyst who founded our day hospital, who never held it against a colleague for leaving it to pursue other interests.

The best form of treatment is that which Bion termed a *working hypothesis* in a group that is concentrated on its object – and finding its economy of object cathexis towards patients – by refocusing on clinical practice and seeking to deepen the knowledge of the patients – their destructive impulses but also their wonderful life impulses, always equally present.

Conclusion

The new therapeutic issues

Symbolisation

Symbolisation constitutes the great challenge in autism, and cognitivists and psychoanalysts agree that it belongs at the heart of the therapeutic issues. Alan Leslie emphasises that access to meta-representations is the essential stage to be crossed.

Marion Milner

Among psychoanalysts, we are indebted to René Roussillon for bringing Marion Milner's work into favour in France. A painter herself, she took an interest in impediments to creative work, and her work is unusual in having inspired Winnicott. Her 1952 article 'The role of illusion in symbol formation'[1] provides a remarkable description of a child therapy in which she realises that the Kleinian interpretations neglect an essential aspect of what is happening for her patient and in her countertransference.

Criticising Jones's view of symbolisation as a process that 'arises from the desire to deal with reality in the easiest possible way, from "the desire for ease and pleasure struggling with the demand of necessity",' she writes: 'Do we really mean that it is only the desire for ease and pleasure, and not necessity, that drives us to identify one thing with another which is in fact not the same? Are we not rather driven by the internal necessity for inner organization, pattern, coherence, the basic need to discover identity in difference without which experience becomes chaos?' (p. 84). This naturally concerns every human being. She nevertheless thinks that Jones implicitly accepted this because in 1916 (only a few years ahead of cognitive research!) he had written: 'there opens up the possibility ... of a theory of scientific discovery, inventions, etc., for psychologically this consists in an overcoming of the resistances that normally prevent regression towards the infantile unconscious tendency to note identity in differences' (pp. 84–85).

Milner makes the connection between the primitive activity of

---

[1] Milner, M. The role of illusion in symbol formation. In: *The Suppressed Madness of Sane Men*. London: Tavistock, 1987, pp. 83–113.

symbolism in civilisation and the work of poetry – which Wordsworth describes as finding the familiar in the unfamiliar. She adds: 'the word illusion is also needed because this word does imply that there is a relation to an external object of feeling, even though a phantastic one, since the person producing the fusion believes that the secondary object *is* the primary one' (p. 87). She then considers the way in which her young patients concentrate at particular times. 'I have often noticed, when in contact with children playing, that there occurs now and then a particular type of absorption in what they are doing, which gives the impression that something of great importance is going on' (pp. 87–88). She explains that beyond the psychoanalytic works that demonstrate the normal child's curiosity about his parents' or his own sexual organs, it should be taken into account that 'the primary "object" that the infant seeks to find again is a fusion of self and object, it is mouth and breast felt as fused into one. Thus the concept of fusion is present, both in the primary situation, between self and object, and in the secondary one, between the new situation and the old one' (p. 88).

In her theory of normal development, Milner shows us a fusion at work that will then be able to form a link in temporality. Is this a psychic crossroads at which the normal child displays a healthy *adhesive identity* in Esther Bick's sense, as distinct from the pathological adhesive identification, the clinging, described by Donald Meltzer?

Autistic symptomatology often essentially constitutes a concentration that is no longer merely intense but absolute. Milner in any case attributes to good teachers the capacity to find the 'moments when the "original" poet in each of us created the outside world for us, by finding the familiar in the unfamiliar', moments that are usually forgotten by the subject or 'guarded in some secret place of memory because they were too much like visitations of the gods to be mixed with everyday thinking' (p. 88). These are teachers who know how to inspire the imagination, so that a subject or an art are illuminated with meaning.

The psychoanalytic setting provides a means of exploring these moments, and Milner describes the treatment of a child during the wartime bombardments in London. He is playing at bombing a village with matches or flares. However, his treatment of what might appear to be a simple metaphor of the trauma also incorporates some other elements: the child explains that the villagers think the lorries arriving in the analyst's village 'are gods' and he introduces a 'Mrs Noah' figure. At the end of the session, he plays with some molten wax and smears some of it on his analyst's thumbs, saying that he is 'double-jointed' and asking if she is too, which the analyst initially interprets as an expression of bisexuality. He had previously sought complete control by bringing a Meccano set with which 'you can make *anything*'. Some difficulties at school begin to be represented in the treatment through a game in which the child takes the role of a sadistic schoolmaster and for days and sometimes weeks the analyst had to write out 'lines' if she talked and everything that she did as requested was scorned and denigrated. For me, this brings back many memories of treating neurotic children! One of the children with whom I was working made me do some drawings with my eyes closed and follow his instructions (with very mediocre results!) in order to assuage his need for control, transforming me into a blind robot. He nevertheless must have identified with his psychoanalyst because he wrote to me much later to tell me that he was embarking on some studies – in medicine.

Milner observed that the tyrannical tone was immediately abandoned when the child started to play with a toy. In relation to toys, she then developed her theory of the *pliable medium*, in which it is possible to discover a form of activity that is halfway between day-dreaming and direct muscular activity applied to a living object. This provides an excellent description of Winnicott's concept of transitional space, in which the attempt to discover whether the object is created or found in external reality has to be abandoned. Her patient was then able to accept the activities of a school photography club as something enjoyable and Milner understood this development as an indication that he had ceased to regard school life as an incarnation of 'not-me-ness'. She recalled that at the beginning of the war, the child had experienced the disappearance of his father when he was called up and the simultaneous disappearance of his most valued toy, a woolly rabbit. She thought that this loss (of what Winnicott has since termed the 'transitional object') had been very important and that her own role in the sessions was that of the lost rabbit. 'He so often treated me as totally his own to do what he liked with, as though I were dirt, his dirt, or as a tool, an extension of his own hand. (He had never been a thumb sucker.)' He constantly reprimanded her for imaginary lateness. 'In fact it certainly did seem that for a very long time he did need to have the illusion that I was part of himself' (p. 94).

Reading this account of a child who is not autistic, it is striking to observe the flexible representation of the implacable problematics to which Birger Sellin refers in autism, in which the capacity for shared illusion is tragically lacking.

I would also emphasise something that is absent from both Milner's and Winnicott's considerations, which is how many demands are made on the masochism of therapists in order to be able to tolerate the patient's sadistic attacks 'without a change towards retaliation' (1969, p. 714).[2] For Winnicott, the capacity to survive without taking revenge constitutes the deepest driving force of the therapeutic action. This applies even more with an autistic patient, as Judy Barron would readily confirm. However, the psychic economy at work in the analyst – the caregiver or the parent – which it seems to me can only be masochistic in nature – has the significance of connecting the child's life and death drives, fusing them in the service of life, as Benno Rosenberg has emphasised.

Let us return to Milner, who quotes Scott to explain the game with boundaries. He takes up Winnicott's idea that a 'good enough' mother enables her child's predisposition to hallucinate a good situation to become fused with the earliest sensations of this situation. It is therefore like an 'oscillation between the illusion of union and the fact of contact, which is another way of describing the discovery of an *interface*, a boundary, or a place of contact, and perhaps at the same time is another way of describing the discovery of "the me" and "the you" ' (p. 95, my italics). He then comments that evil union and evil contact are equally necessary. Even more interesting here is a comment about situations in which interfaces are eliminated, which he calls 'cosmic bliss' and 'catastrophic chaos'. As examples of this, he quotes situations in which a face can be either extremely beautiful or utterly ugly. There again, autism resonates with these descriptions. In an endnote, Milner explains that for Winnicott this concept of union presupposes a regression after which the union has become thinkable. Before this, he states, 'there's union but no *idea* of union, and here the terms good and bad have no function' (p. 112).

Milner herself wonders how we can know whether, in these states, the skin contains the entire world – which seems to her to deny the skin – and refers to the oceanic feeling described by Freud (fusion with nature as a whole) and, with chaos, to a schizophrenic adult patient who felt that she could no longer keep the world out, which was agonising for her. She then remembers that her young patient sometimes played at creating a magic spectacle with light and fire into which he then had to put in one of his lead soldiers to melt as a sacrificial figure, which was staged in an enchantingly beautiful way. It seemed to her that he was thereby showing that in the metal cup he used he was representing his internal integration of destructive forces – also the fire of Eros – and the fantasy of passionate

[2] The use of an object. *International Journal of Psychoanalysis*, 50: 711–716.

union with the external object. In fact, she states almost explicitly here that there is a drive fusion opening the way to the object relationship. There is also the creation of a new entity in the fusion of the various elements that go into the 'fire cup'. Also, the little boy had interests that were usual for his age and he apologised, for example, for the 'childish' quality of one of his dreams.

I remember having melted some lead myself as a child. As it melts, a metal liquid that is as shiny as silver and as bright as mercury emerges from the scorias of oxidation. It feels as if an alchemy is taking place ... how do children today gain access to the phantasmagorias of fire? [3]

After this, the young boy lost his inhibition about drawing and became capable of artistic productions.

Milner emphasises the need for a medium between self-created reality and external reality, illustrating the aphorism 'Art creates Nature' (p. 99). This medium must be pliable and her young patient illustrated this by telling her one day that she was a gas or that he would have to dissolve her down or evaporate her until she became one. For her, art – for what is felt – and science – for what is perceived – sets out to reduce the distance between the available means of expression and emotional experiences or an understanding of the world.

Drawing on her countertransference, Milner makes an observation that is very important for the analysis of difficult cases with a negative therapeutic reaction (when the patient cannot tolerate healing): the boy's analysis changed when she challenged her own fundamental conception of this treatment by considering that he was not in a purely defensive deep regression in treating her as his gas, his breath or his faeces, but in 'an essential recurrent phase in the development of a creative relation to the world'; 'the boy then gradually became able to allow the external object, represented by me, to exist in its own right' (p. 104).

Let us draw from this treatment of a child who was much better structured than an autistic child this understanding of the tyranny that we have so often encountered in our journey through autism, and this lesson that we must expect to be exposed to a deep internal change in our convictions and our theories if psychic change is to emerge. If psychoanalysts were to abandon the maternal aetiology of autism and cognitivists were to abandon their denial of affect and the drives, for instance, this would form a good starting-point.

---

3 It may be that this contributes to the appeal of tobacco in later life, with its smoke that not only generates shapes that isolate and protect the smoker from the otherness of the world but permeates it with the smoker's own smell.

René Roussillon

In his book *Paradoxes et situations limites de la psychanalyse* [Paradoxes and borderline situations in psychoanalysis],[4] Roussillon uses the example of modelling clay to illustrate how a pliable medium transforms actions into signs that can become meaningful and how, in this representational activity, it is the representational capacity itself that is represented. This meta-representation is the very essence of the symbolisation process.

Indestructibility is another essential characteristic of the pliable medium. As I commented to René Roussillon, when treating autistic children there is no real question of modelling with the clay: instead of using it to shape imaginary food to eat and containers to put it in, the children eat it! Even in treating neurotic children, it often ends up encrusted in the office carpet or dried up after being mixed together many times over, leaving it a pretty goose-dropping colour, as it proves more sensitive to the ageing process than it appears. However, he is fundamentally right, for the modelling clay concerned is ourselves, as 'good enough clay', we hope, to allow ourselves to be 'used' in Winnicott's positive sense, capable of transforming the traces of wounds inflicted by patients into a story. When we are pulled out of shape or the psychic framework that we give to our care institution is stretched, this hurts us, and it is important that we do not loosen our hold, that we abandon neither the patient nor our hope and without seeking undue revenge, 'without a change towards retaliation' (1969, p. 714). It is not enough to survive the destructiveness; like the primary object for a child with a gift for life, we must also then show ourselves to be 'creative and living', as Roussillon emphasises in a more recent work, *Agonie, clivage et symbolisation* [Agony, splitting and symbolisation].[5]

As the result of the fusion of the life drives and the death drives of our masochism, then put in the service of psychic life, it becomes possible to exercise a containing function in Bion's sense: gathering together on a weekly basis, an institution has to tackle the difficult – remarkable or intense – moments of the week, to link together and synthesise actions that are meaningless in isolation, when scattered between the various participants, but which can become meaningful if they are placed in connection as part of a story. To our recurrent surprise, so strange is life, the child that we have talked about on a Friday afternoon is often a very

[4] Paris, PUF, 1991 (page numbers refer to this edition – quotations translated).

[5] Paris, PUF, 1999.

different one on Monday morning! In the containing function, the countertransference is a symbolising matrix.

In his work on symbolisation, Roussillon emphasises its essential aspects. Taking up the importance Winnicott accorded to the destruction of the object, he suggests that we consider the *destroyed/found* of the object as an experience that is just as possible as the *created/found*. This may account for the inner aspects of the potential for mutilation in cases, unfortunately possible, in which the object is psychically unavailable and therefore cannot contradict destruction. Bion's *attack on linking* is thus understood as a repetition of this damaging experience. Depression in the mother, or boredom or despair on the part of the therapist, would then reinforce the primary failure.

Hatred, however, has to find its place in an active ambivalence, and indifference, which is the more fatal in my view, should not be confused with resentment or hostility, which already or still bespeak love. 'The object 'survives'; it is 'discovered' as an object of the drive; it is loved. At the same time, however, the subject depends on it; the object can be absent or deficient and be hated accordingly', states Roussillon (p. 177). This is why a theory of love and the object relationship, to use J. M. Vidal's term, precedes a theory of other minds.

The path of symbolisation belongs to the primary object as the first entity, as Roussillon emphasises here, both *to be symbolised* and *for symbolising*. This also provides a better explanation of the tendency of psychoanalysts naïvely to conflate the *subjective* object created by the child's psyche with the psyche of the real person who enables him to find an embodiment of his creation in reality, as well as the internal future of this more or less felicitous encounter that forms the basis of external reality *for the child*. In a normal psyche, this hybrid is all that will later be found and the psychoanalyst will have to work on this internal reality. In relation to autism, it may be easier to disentangle this cross-fertilisation of internal and external that modern psychoanalysis has instigated by considering structural psychic abnormalities as indications of disorders in psychic construction or the history of previous generations. This pathology shows us in fact that the child can also be incapable, if he is lacking in creative potentialities, of creating his mother. The encounter thus fails because of him and this is a desperately helpless little god who fails to create the world and remains stranded on the shores of psychic birth. This would explain the rejection by their child attested by some mothers. Fundamentally, it is the child's good health that Winnicott idealised. Many cases that we have outlined demonstrate the combination of two components, which is manifest for example when a child's pathology involves a separation that deprives him of maternal and paternal support.

To return to Roussillon's work on symbolisation in general and the defining characteristics of the pliable medium: to the plasticity, transformability and indestructibility that Milner emphasises, Roussillon adds its perceptibility – which enables it to be controlled by motoricity and leads the way to play – availability, reliability and constancy, which safeguard against loss. These characteristics are then transferred to the symbolising capacity itself having been adequately tested, including in their limitations, allowing their subjective appropriation. This concept of experimentation with the shared illusion and its limitations – harshness and its masculine quality have to be encountered there – explains the time-span of shared life necessary for a therapeutic resumption or discovery of this progression. Here, therapists themselves must be accorded a necessary capacity for creative illusion in the framework of their action.

Roussillon condemns a naïve, albeit attractive, theory of primary symbolisation – which is in my view the real issue for research into autism. He takes up the distinction between thing-representations and words-representations, which makes it possible to identify two stages of symbolisation. We have seen that literal interpretation leads to a one-to-one correspondence between a word and a thing, preventing any generalisation in autism for cognitivists. The issue is an important one. We must therefore seek to understand it more deeply. The thing-representation is not self-evident. It presupposes a differentiation between the hallucination and the thing-representation that can exist internally in the absence of the perception of the thing. Some have thus considered that a *foundational mourning* was a precondition of access to the absence of the thing. This is an attractive idea to anyone who is familiar with the adhesiveness in autism and its consequent prohibition of any distance and therefore any mourning, which presupposes thinking about absence. Elaborating the absence of the primary object thus seems to be a prerequisite for the representational capacity.

However, Roussillon denies us this radical explanation for the disturbances in symbolisation in autism by emphasising the circular temporal paradox in this proposition: there is no possibility of mourning if a representational capacity is not present, and a high-level capacity! Mourning implies the representation of absence and representation would involve the presence of the capacity for mourning.

The author might be criticised for condemning a paradox here despite his earlier enthusiasm for paradox and its psychic productiveness. We might introduce a maternal or therapeutic solution of a psychic support for the object to escape this aporia. Symbolisation would thus result from a *psychic graft*, bearing witness to the contribution of civilisation to the construction of the human mind. The maternal or therapeutic capacities for symbolising absence and mourning for the primary unity would provide an escape from the vicious circle of the incapacity for mourning/deficiency in symbolisation, providing a way out of the circularity in order to accede to a progredient state in which each possibility is reinforced by the other. This would also account for the therapeutic efficacy of the day hospital setting through its work on the purely temporary absence of the parents that does not signify their loss. It would also explain access to the operativity of that which Meltzer terms a four-dimensional temporality in order to foster its onset, and this parental psychic contribution would certainly be a wonderful gift: time. This would also provide a coherent explanation of the (indisputable) pathogenic effects of severe maternal depression; not only in terms of the difficulty of cathexis but more specifically through the paralysis of mourning capacities that are effectively bypassed where depression is present.

If I had been writing fifty years ago, I would have been fairly content to stop here. However, this theory – despite its interesting insight into the pathogenic effects of postpartum depression – reminds us that autism cannot be conceived according to this model and that once again there is a risk of considering only the flaws in the external support while idealising the child's good health in turn. However, we should not throw out the therapeutic idea of a 'graft of mourning' with the aetiological bathwater.

Therefore, let us follow Roussillon's rejection of this aporia that will restore that which is internal to the child to its place. Between the lived experience and its symbolisation there is in fact for him a temporal gap that is a requirement of the living being. He emphasises that symbolisation is concerned with the paradox that something similar is simultaneously different and that it enables us to live by changing while remaining ourselves, similar and different at the same time (like the dog seen from the front and in profile to which Frith refers). This symbolically connects symbolisation and identity, and we can understand the relevance of this link in autism. 'The symbol both does and does not resemble itself; this is in fact its defining characteristic ... it always applies to something other than what it designates. The space or domain that it defines is thus the only one that can receive and tackle the paradox of the living being in his process of perpetual change' (p. 220).

Roussillon suggests a return to the child's early animism, which confers life on what is inanimate beyond him. '*As he hallucinates himself in objects, psychic processes that are inherently non-material and imperceptible assume a perceptible and material form, and can be represented and located: the psyche can begin to comprehend them through their materialised form ... Through perception, the psychic material takes shape, through the hallucination the perceptible material comes alive; through motoricity it becomes transformable*' (p. 224, my italics).

Let us digress slightly in order to emphasise that this theory implies a capacity for projection into a recognised external world or into the intermediate transitional space, both internal and external, in which it is also involved. As we have seen, both these capacities are lacking in autistic children. However, this explains the therapeutic importance of creating appropriate scenes for this 'externalisation', for example in psychodrama or in a theatre group, and of these being brought to life by therapists using their transitional capacities.

Confronted with the otherness of the object or the space into which it is projected, the psychic material then retreats into the inner space through an internalisation. In this process, the detour by the object is accompanied by psychic transformations carried out within it that will bear its imprint. The projection is thus followed by an introjection and we find here in Roussillon the exchanges that Bion describes in the *capacity for maternal reverie*, which also presuppose introjective capacities for identification.

Roussillon thus joins the debate here to summon the 'objeux' of the poet Francis Ponge – a term also used by Pierre Fédida. Serving the unfolding of auto-subjective play, these also enable play itself and its process to be constituted as an object; the time of meta-representation is found there. By making it possible simultaneously to represent by projection the object's first response but also everything that has been refused or proved unobtainable from it, the utilisation and its support, for Roussillon play already contains 'a first expression of the incest taboo'. Auto-erotisms play a part in this: however, play 'is not pure auto-erotism or self-sensuality; it is the auto-erotic activity that paves the way to symbolisation, which shifts self-sensuality forward from itself to open its way to the object, to symbolise its otherness and thus to recognise at the same time that it is reduced by its actual representation. However, this is its limitation; play remains dependent on the presence and materiality of the *objeu*, it remains injurious to primary narcissism in the very extent of this dependence. It provides a way of understanding the material of being, but at the risk of imprisoning the symbolisation of the latter in a form that threatens to fetishise it, to fix it in this very form. *It presents the limit of what it is proposing; it materialises but threatens imprisonment in the material and form that it confers*' (p. 231).

It should be noted that Winnicott himself had touched on the risk of fetishising the transitional object in his famous article, rejecting it in the first version, but adding a clinical case – the child with the string – to illustrate this in the second edition of *Playing and Reality*.[6] Roussillon later emphasised the dematerialisation of primary symbolisation that is later attested by dreams.

With these modern theories of symbolisation, I have sought to demonstrate the full complexity and abundance of the process at work, which leaves us with a vast field of research if we are to foster the onset of symbolisation in autism. If this brings the psychic disasters of autism back into the foreground by measuring the distance to be travelled, this nevertheless gives some grounds for hope. Roussillon in fact offers us a new paradox – a valuable one this time – for abandoning any pessimism that might arise from an adult theory that projects our own thinking categories on to psychic birth.

I have often been struck by the absence of repression in my young patients, whose resulting inhuman behaviours sometimes make them resemble monsters. In fact, postulating the absence of what Freud termed 'primal' repression seems to deny any possibility of structural progress and, as we have seen, on each occasion the testimonies have refuted this pessimism. Roussillon gives us the valuable explanation here that the primal (structurally) is not the same as the primary, the earliest (temporally). It is only in deferred action that the primal is constructed as a founder of identity, as the history of nations, which acquire identity symbols retrospectively, clearly demonstrates. It is after a victory that a particular event takes on a primal value, for example, as the 14 July illustrates for the French Republic. Piera Aulagnier has given a useful account of this process in psychic construction.

In his work on primary symbolisation, Roussillon takes the view that in this process a trace must disappear and that it then constitutes an element of the primal repressed material, as a product of symbolisation: 'The symbolisation of an experience represses in its very process the trace of the unsymbolised experience that it symbolises; it simultaneously inscribes and loses it. This operation gives rise to the "primal repression" that emerges as the product of symbolisation' (p. 239).

---

[6] 1971, London, Tavistock.

This inversion of cause and effect is remarkable because we have observed how theories of autism are always drawn, as if by contagion, towards a simplistic, linear causality, as if the autistic problematic led inexorably down this path. Here it is the reverse that occurs: instead of considering the lack of primal repression as the cause of the inability to symbolise, it becomes the result. This means that every advance in the symbolisation process is accompanied by a negativation or repression of the constitution of an organising nucleus of repressed material, *originating* an organisation of psychic life!

Semiotics

Two authors have recently addressed the subject of autism with reference to linguistics: Pierre Delion and Laurent Danon-Boileau.

Pierre Delion

Pierre Delion's extensive clinical experience, including in institutional care, led to a book about the institutional psychotherapy practice that he established in Angers. From a perspective based on Lacanian theory and an institutional psychotherapy practice affiliated to the work of François Tosquelles and Jean Oury, he demonstrates in these seminars[7] a method of using the day hospital as a psychotherapeutic tool that often concurs by different means with my own practice, which is inspired by the works of Philippe Paumelle, Serge Lebovici, René Diatkine and Paul-Claude Racamier. In setting up the day hospital that I run today, Francine Klein had also drawn inspiration from Michel Soulé and Roger Misès. In his day hospital for adults in the 13th arrondissement in Paris, Jacques Azoulay had also taught me a rigorous way of conducting institutional psychotherapy.

Beyond the divergences in psychoanalytic theory, the post-war resurgence in French psychiatry – a rebellion against the tragedy in which 30–40,000 mentally ill people starved to death in psychiatric hospitals during the German occupation – that favoured greater integration in living with other city-dwellers, gave rise to a common trend of using institutions for treatment. These values have to be championed today in a context in which psychiatry appears to be reverting to a viewpoint that

[7] *Séminaires sur l'autisme et la psychose infantile* [Seminars on autism and childhood psychosis]. Paris, Érès, 1997.

emphasises the symptom to the detriment of the human being as a complete entity.

In the book based on his thesis,[8] Pierre Delion addresses the emergence of communication between human beings and seeks to turn this into a therapeutic tool. Working from the hypothesis that an autistic child 'communicates his anxieties and the defences that he constructs against them by "means of the body",' he considers it essential to try to decipher these signs in order to be able to reflect to the child some evidence that his message has been received, so that he does not sink any further into a state 'that takes cognisance of an unresponsive world'. It is therefore necessary at first to situate oneself in the non-habitual 'non-Euclidean' spaces, in which the child produces signs in order to receive them, 'then possibly, in certain favourable cases ... to "infer" some significance from them, possibly even finding a meaning there' (pp. 91–92). This is the task of semiotics and Delion returns to his sources in Charles Peirce, whom he quotes here: 'All semiosis is a triadic relationship between a *representamen*, an interpretant and its object ... "A sign, or *representamen*, is something which stands to somebody for something in some respect or capacity. It addresses somebody, that is, creates in the mind of that person an equivalent sign, or perhaps a more developed sign. That sign which it creates I call the *interpretant* of the first sign. The sign stands for something, its *object*" ' (p. 96).[9] It seems likely in fact that this sentence was inspired by Lacan's definition of the signifier.

To explain the use of the terms – *representamen*, interpretant and object: a smile can be interpreted when some results are being received as an enjoyment of success, but in another context as happiness that it has stopped raining. The *representamen* is the sign; the interpretant is not the person who interprets the sign but a constitutive element of the sign itself. The interpretant is something that has to be produced by therapists with autistic patients who cannot produce it themselves.

Delion's open-mindedness to other theories, including post-Kleinian works on autism, encourages him to seek a further connection and parallels between the various concepts that he examines and links as follows – Peirce in fact suggests three categories:

Firstness – 'being of the positive qualitative possibility' (the *primal*

---

[8] *L'enfant autiste, le bébé et la sémiotique* [Autistic children, babies and semiotics]. Paris, PUF, 2000 (page numbers refer to this edition – quotations are translated).

[9] Logic as semiotic: the theory of signs. In *Philosophical Writings of Charles S. Peirce*, edited by J. Buchler, New York, Dover Publications, 1955, p. 99.

register in psychoanalysis), which Deledalle defines as follows: 'Firstness is the category of feeling or emotion or, more precisely, proto-emotion, the experience that is not considered, not even felt as it is lived' (p. 98). This is what Erwin Straus terms the 'pathic moment' of feeling, which precedes perception and being in the world. Delion associates this firstness with the *contact* described in terms of adhesive identifications (p. 101) and with the *sensations* in Frances Tustin's theory, which simultaneously submerge the psychic apparatus before it can transform them into perceptions and representations and serve to protect it from fears of annihilation. The baby's hunger provides an illustration of this register. In firstness, the object in Peirce's sense, namely the referent to which the interpretant refers the *representamen*, is the *icon* (characterised by resemblance, as the map resembles the land). Interactions here are affective.

Secondness: this is 'the incarnation of the actual event' (p. 101), action in the raw state, the being of the actual event (the *primary* register). Hunger is now incarnated, situated in the body by the baby and felt in the actual. The object becomes an *index* (the smoke that indicates an actual fire that I cannot see). This can be connected with the register of projective identification (the paranoiac will think that car is red in order to pretend he is a revolutionary...) and *metonymy* can be summoned. Interactions are behavioural.

Thirdness: the being of the law that will govern future events (*secondary* register). 'This represents the effort of abstraction that the human mind can make in order, based on sensations experienced in firstness, which are felt and "deposited" in the body, to draw from this some form of thought with which it will construct a psychic apparatus that has among its original features "thinking thoughts". That is to say, the organising potentiality contained in thirdness and its importance as a category in establishing the law' (p. 102). The hungry baby's impatience and the timing of the mother's response become an interaction. 'The object' is now the symbol (the smoke, as a general concept), and it is *metaphor* that will be used. Interactions are fantasmatic.

Semiotics is necessarily triadic, the author points out, because 'there is no unity without limits. A second, beyond this limit, is therefore required for there to be a first. Moreover, it is impossible to form an authentic third by modifying the pair without introducing something of a different nature from the unity and the pair. This something is a third'.

This is as far as I can discuss Delion's work here, which then becomes highly complex as it pursues Peirce's writings. However, he does indicate the importance of the *cross-modal* nature of mother-child interactions (p. 119):

in emotional attunement, the mother responds in a different channel from her child (her voice responds to mimicry). He gives an experience as an example: the interest taken by some children in the institution in a storyteller using sign-language, and therefore 'bimodal', who was attending to a deaf child.

Finally, Delion understands stereotypies in terms of an incapacity to move from the trace to the *tessera* (the organic, bodily trace), which connects in a reflex mode and makes 'an inadvertent link between an emotion, an anxious affect and a communicative intention – even if autism appears to be specifically about non-communication' (p. 135). Stereotypies 'are therefore scar tissue left by an attempt to communicate something with the body' (p. 137).

In conclusion, we can observe a new point of convergence that situates the fundamental issue for autism in the early stages of symbolisation and takes account of the complexity of exchange between human beings. Just as Roussillon emphasises the importance of primary symbolisation and the constitution of the *primal*, Delion emphasises the *firstness* that describes its register. His reference to Peirce's work demonstrates the level of complexity with which thought is confronted when describing the preconditions for its emergence.

Laurent Danon-Boileau

A psychoanalyst and linguistician, Laurent Danon-Boileau has a keen interest in language and he developed an interest in autism through his treatment of dysphasic children, to which he refers in *The Silent Child*.[10] His encounter with autism inspired some reflections on the useful strategy for establishing contact that he outlines in *Children Without Language: From Dysphasia to Autism*.[11] His technique places a strong emphasis on introducing a play dimension into the relationship, precisely because this is lacking in autism, showing some affinities with René Diatkine's practice, which combines a constant search for the unexpected with a patient, attentive listening that respects the child's pace.

Danon-Boileau suggests linking psychoanalytic, linguistic and cognitive knowledge to conceive a form of language acquisition freed from the

[10] Oxford University Press, 2002, translated by Kevin Windle (*L'Enfant qui ne disait rien*, Paris, Odile Jacob, 1995).

[11] Oxford University Press, 2006, translated by James Grieve (*Des enfants sans langage*, Paris, Odile Jacob, 2002).

obligatory stages and certainties of each field in order to take account of 'the unpredictable diversity of the ways that lead to language' (pp. 4–5). The complete opposition between the cognitive theory of an instrumental lack in the child's equipment and the psychoanalytic theory that this is entirely a defence does not seem pertinent to him. He therefore rejects the stark opposition between the psychoanalytic therapeutic method – interpretation and making sense – and that of the cognitive therapist – re-education or remediation.

This author also refers to some cognitive experiments demonstrating the existence of cross-modal innate knowledge, as the experiment with the two nipples shows. A rough nipple on a baby's bottle that is full of milk and a smooth nipple on an empty bottle are offered to the child to explore with his mouth while his eyes are covered. When he is shown the two bottles afterwards, he immediately turns to the rough nipple on the full bottle. This demonstrates that this baby has the capacity for 'converting the perception of a feeling of roughness into a visual version of the same information' (p. 207). Danon-Boileau points out that 'Some cognitivists take the view that this tells us something about the way our recognition of objects in the outside world functions', and adds: 'To me, it shows one of the ways in which signs are established: the rough nipple can be shown to someone else's eyes as a sign of sensations inside the mouth. Through this association, one contrives to signify to others a feeling they are not experiencing. Something that is internal, unrepresentable, and incommunicable in itself becomes associated with an external perception that plays the part of a signifier and makes the feeling accessible to others' (p. 207). However, a second condition is necessary: 'to make a sign, I must be able to think that the connection I make between signifier and signified has the same meaning for the person to whom I am addressing it' (p. 207). The capacity of the baby, who spontaneously knows how to stick out his tongue, to do so in the mirror in a developing game of alternation when someone sticks out their tongue at him shows the early capacity for this, which paves the way for all imitative games.

Danon-Boileau defines himself as a practitioner of 'psychoanalytical semiotherapy' in therapeutic situations with children who do not communicate. 'In communication, any child who cannot interpret the signs being addressed to him is constantly being thrust into the unforeseeable. This causes the terror and extreme agitation to which withdrawal is a response ... converting an instrumental disorder into self-defense, much as a deaf person copes with a malfunctioning hearing aid by switching it off, preferring total silence to partial understanding. The defect in the equipment lies at the origin of agitation or withdrawal. But it is the reinforcement of the defect itself that is the first defense chosen by the subject' (p. 214).

Danon-Boileau subscribes to Meltzer's theory of dismantling here, but considers that this predominantly applies to the radical dissociation of sensation from perception, whereas the 'connection between these two faculties is essential to the establishment of signs and the ability to communicate' (p. 221). He indicates that internal bodily sensations must take shape in representations born of the contents of visual or auditory perceptions. From this viewpoint, stereotypy can be conceived as a 'failed attempt at self-cure' (p. 225) because the author points out that the child who moves his hand across his eyes is not merely discharging the excitation and expelling a tension that may have been created by the presence of other people. He is also associating the internal bodily sensations in his wrist with the alternation of shade and light before his eyes. Similarly, the child who repeatedly drops an object is linking the muscular sensation in his hand with his perceptions as he sees it falling and hears the sound of the impact. 'Stereotypy is an attempt at mastering sensations that have become unrepresentable through their severance from the perceptible. If this link is not stabilized, if sensations cannot be durably associated with perception, then all sensation must forever remain in a limbo from which there is no access to representation or affect and where the only way of controlling it is to repeat it' (p. 226).

Subverting the repetition in the encounter with the child by introducing a surprise element that momentarily makes the other person exist helps to turn the stereotypy into a game. Danon-Boileau in fact refuses to consider the barriers between the normal and pathological registers as fixed, permanent and impenetrable. In common with Winnicott, he further claims 'that in-depth psychotherapy can be conducted without interpretive accompaniment' (p. 75). While refraining from any misguided pedagogical zeal, he seeks 'to let the child (re)claim the role of a subject with something meaningful to say' (p. 80). As he offers a simplified mirror of the child's spontaneous activities or prolongs them himself, over weeks, a game of alternation starts to develop and the author allows it to become established in the repetition and the child's experience of his game being cathected by the therapist, who then goes on to create some discrepancies: the child has thus developed successive phases of his game, a succession about which some knowledge is shared by the two protagonists. One phase thus becomes a sign that heralds the next: speech can start to punctuate the stages that accentuate this communication. However, the child's effort at representation leads him to confront a discrepancy between that which he anticipated and that which actually occurs. With an indubitable talent of his own for teasing, the author thus goes on to vary some of his responses and to introduce into a ritual accentuated by certain words a word that goes on for ever … and is then suddenly interrupted. For example, he might blow on a little car instead of pushing it in the usual way. 'By slightly inflecting an accustomed practice, one can sometimes help bring about a representation requiring words' (p. 83).

The abnormality of time

This question posed by Birger Sellin's text, a less familiar one than that of space, seems to merit further investigation. The first author to contemplate a temporal abnormality in autism was a science-fiction writer, Philip K. Dick, who experienced psychotic states and experimented with drugs. In 1964, in *Martian Time-Slip*,[12] the author imagines that an autistic person lives in a faster temporal mode, which isolates him but enables him to produce, in drawings, an image of the future of the planet. As we have seen, the extreme rapidity of certain responses seems to indicate a subcortical processing of information that bypasses complex cortical elaboration.

Work on symbolisation has shown us a temporality that is necessary to its process, just as thought unfolds in time, whereas Temple Grandin's *thinking in pictures* is a series of static scenes. Rosenberg suggests that primal masochism involves the ability to wait for satisfaction, thus the capacity to erotise unpleasure, without which the hallucinatory satisfaction cannot unfold. Thus, the emergence of the first temporality depends on a kernel of masochism that internally accomplishes the first possible fusion of the life and death drives and the organisation of a rudimentary ego. With the tyranny of the autistic child, we have discovered the apparently essential requirement not only for clinging but for having 'everything, all at once', which seems to be highly restrictive. The inability to wait may therefore result from this failure of masochism. This is why the emergence of masochistic capacities in contact between children seems to me to be a positive development (compared with the absence of relations), even if some care should be taken to prevent it from becoming extreme.

In *The Bipersonal Field: Experiences in Child Analysis*,[13] Antonino

[12] New York, Ballantine.

[13] London, Routledge 1999.

Ferro developed an original psychoanalytic theory that emphasises the importance of creating an account or narrative of emotional experience. In accordance with Bion, whose ideas he extends in a very lively and lucid way, he considers psychoanalysis as a creative encounter. He takes up Madeleine and Willy Baranger's concept of a psychoanalytic *field* created in the treatment by participation between the two psyches of patient and analyst, which allows the identification of specific resistances, *bastions* that arise from the defensive collusion of the two protagonists. This theory of analysis criticises the closed interpretive systems that can sometimes occur in Kleinian technique in order to promote unsaturated interpretations that allow the patient's creativity to emerge. The importance of narrativity clearly calls on the self-evidence of the temporal dimension and the register of symbolisation in its connection with representation. However, it is also the space of the play in sessions that is privileged. This procedure contains a highly significant emphasis on the interaction in the transference and countertransference, with a strong requirement for authenticity in treating autistic patients, where the dimension of psychic creation is essential, with strong participation from the analyst's psychic apparatus.

Lateral and adhesive perception

What lessons can be drawn from the testimonies, which concur with regard to lateral, or adhesive, instantaneous and total perception in some autistic people?

Certain lessons have already been learnt from reassessing the help provided to autistic people in teaching and valuable supplements to this without reference to their expressive capacities, skills or wishes in a way that excludes them from psychically nurturing activities. Placing children together in treatment settings at an early age provides a relatively easy way of achieving this by selecting the constitution of heterogeneous groups. It is more difficult to implement this for low-achieving older children and it is a new challenge to avoid depriving them of stimulation without also creating artificial and meaningless situations. But how can this be done?

In any case, this certainly cannot be done by maintaining a senseless alternative between schooling and treatment for children who are achieving, since the two can be combined!

As we have seen, there is a need to open new lines of research in order to explore the paradoxical reading capacities, even to bring these out, and not only through facilitated communication. Cognitive studies might seek to identify some signs that would foster therapeutic efforts to good effect.

Some avenues

What has been learnt from formerly autistic people concerning the benefits of being accompanied in interests that involve these atypical modes of functioning gives me some grounds for hope from attempts to use information processing methods that are akin to this type of functioning.

I recently bought a digital camera for the day hospital in the desire – not yet realised for lack of time – to see if children who were apparently fairly impervious to exchange would be interested in immediately available captures of fragments of reality, achieving the equivalent of adhesive functioning. This experiment could not be done using a Polaroid camera because the photograph contains chemicals from the developing process and I imagine that if these productions were to interest the children, they would have to be left available to them and to be harmless if eaten ... Is this the case with printer ink?

Some children are highly dexterous with video and play extracts from films at their parents' houses. This has led to the suggestion that putting the clips that are skimmed through back into sequence might become a meaningful process and emerge from a form of psychic editing by the child. It might be beneficial that a digital device could draw out this 'editing' by the child, even inspire him to do this, based on sequences of actions in which he has felt involved or that are prototypical of human relations.

I have observed that the computer software at the day hospital that is of greatest interest to autistic people imprisoned in their own universe is ... the screensaver on the computer in the secretarial office! It generates a shape that constantly changes of its own accord. Who might be able to develop 'games' that would materialise a stereotypy that the children would initially be able to change, for example by touching a screen so as to be able to dispense with a keyboard? What shapes would interest them? What developments of these shapes might become meaningful for them: fusions, separations, destruction, organisation or disorganisation of chaos? Would it be interesting to modify these shapes with sounds, cries or words?

We know that some children are able to cathect written material before they acquire language and I have often thought that this enabled them to bypass the obligation to assume the subject position of the speaker, as well as affects conveyed by the voice. However, this also allows the message to be immediately understood, whereas speech imposes a temporality in expression. Roussillon makes a useful observation here by emphasising that writing is a 'visual materialisation of the word': the word-representation turns into a thing-representation. Perhaps this resolves the difficulty of the connection between the thing-representation and the word-representation (secondary symbolisation) or the difficulty of primary symbolisation? We would in any case need to know if language acquisition is compromised by developing substitutes for linguistic communication through pictograms or, rather, if access to communication tested out in that way would enable it to develop.

The political challenges

It must be acknowledged that much remains to be done and that research, psychotherapeutic and educational treatments and specialised education need to be brought together in the pursuit of autonomy and scholastic integration. The implications of this should be considered and the treatment of autistic patients should not be confined to community health institutions, certainly not unless they are provided with therapeutic methods. It should also be remembered that early prevention and treatment are the responsibility of the care system and that parents' associations cannot be expected simultaneously to battle for the future of children who are too often left in their sole charge and to concern themselves with providing means for others to have a better chance than their own child by receiving earlier treatment.

Screening for genetic anomalies should be carried out in all institutions for children and adults that accept mentally handicapped people, and this also therefore applies to autistic patients. This represents a huge task that could be an opportunity for all patients to make a contribution.

In my view, psychiatry should not jettison the treatment of highly anxious autistic adults and clearly not by means of an asylum – for which it is impossible to see a justification in any case, I would observe to parents who reject psychiatry. We need to invent original forms of treatment that take account of psychic characteristics without creating silent ghettoes for low-functioning autists. These might be partnerships that allow specialist intervention in teams working in community health or the maintenance of sufficient time from psychiatrists despite the low scheduling in their demography. However, there is no lack of clinical psychologists to treat the suffering of patients and teams here, and the problem therefore remains entirely a budgetary one.

A highly intelligent part-time care organisation was developed by the director of a special day school, Catherine Alier;[14] this consists in accepting fairly low-achieving adolescents in the daytime and allowing them to board for one week in three, in alternation. During this brief period of separation, the adolescents still have the continuity of the day school. It is thus against a background in which continuity is maintained that a discontinuity can operate with its beneficial psychic effects. This period provides the family with some breathing space and the opportunity to rediscover other modes of functioning. This seems to me highly preferable to the enforced alternative between moving away from home for longer periods and leading a child's life at home. This part-time arrangement deserves to gain widespread acceptance.

Another public health issue arises from the discovery of the progress that can result from working on non-verbal interaction with children who are severely handicapped by neurological or sensory problems and who have developed organisations with autistic components. They too would benefit a great deal from psychic treatments and much remains to be done to give them access to these. My colleagues from community health centres for young children[15] encounter great difficulties in finding institutions to accept children whom they have treated up to the age of six years.

Registered with the catchment area for state child psychiatry that is responsible for patients in the 12th arrondissement in Paris, our day hospital for young children favours their applications. This is only logical. However, what can we do when we know that there is no institution for early treatment in each sector? A waiting list for those outside the sector leaves many requests for treatment unmet every year.

We also have immense difficulty now finding in Paris, which is supposedly overprovided with forms of treatment, colleagues who can accept non-achieving autistic patients or those with associated organic pathologies. The generous Creton amendment, which prohibits throwing out adolescents, without any subsequent solution at the adult age, has had the perverse effect of blocking admissions, with a knock-on effect that has repercussions on those leaving our institution. Should we therefore deprive the youngest patients of early care? When we consider that the earlier treatment begins, the more effective it is?!

---

[14] Director of Alternance Bourg-la-Reine. There is also 'Alternance 75' in Paris. I am indebted to Sophie Châtel for my knowledge of how it operates from her memory of training.

[15] Centres d'action médico-sociale précoce (CAMPS) – community health centres for young children.

On the contrary, a large-scale training programme should be set up so that paediatricians and general practitioners can identify the early signs of autism, namely relational disturbances that can appear as early as one year of age, as opposed to specific autistic symptoms that only emerge later. Unfortunately we still see parents today who have had to do battle with their doctors to obtain recognition of the disorders they have felt to exist in their children! Although the plan for regional diagnostic centres has some relevance here, it is absurd that they cannot combine these with a continuous psychic treatment over several years, restricted by their medical rationale of 'short stays'. This further distorts their perception of the autistic problematic. As Asperger previously said, it is by living with a child that you truly get to know him.

A dream

Several years ago, confronted with these difficulties, I had the idea of an institution for older autistic children. The draft plan that we formulated with the director then of CAMPS, which is also administered by *Entraide universitaire* (along with thirty-four other establishments and community health centres and our day hospital) could not be presented to the committee that selects projects in Paris: the priority then was the (genuine) lack of institutions that accepted adolescents.

In my dream, this institution would be organised with three centres available to children and adolescents, to varying degrees according to their needs.

A centre for psychotherapeutic treatment and research would offer individual psychotherapies and psychodrama to patients.[16] It would also provide a synthesising and regulatory role in the institution as a whole with a possibility of supervising the work of the teams. Parental support would be possible there. Speech therapy and psychomotricity would also feature.

An educational centre would work on the emergence into group life and psychic and physical autonomy, as well as integration into life outside. A boarding system based on alternating weeks as conceived by Catherine Alier would be organised there, as well as holiday visits. Artistic activities would be available: painting, music, theatre. Monthly parents' meetings would link the families with the life of the institution.

---

[16] Dr Bernard Touati runs an inspiring psychodrama programme for older autistic adolescents at the association for mental health in the 13th arrondissement in Paris (ASM 13).

A learning centre would link specialist teachers and a research team working on cognition and learning that would be able to provide a continuous form of care. Integration into external schools would be developed as far as possible. There would be some experimentation with facilitated communication, as well as other forms of assistance with exchange.

Of course, child psychiatrists would attend to each patient and his family, and meetings would bring the various participants together with the patient. A paediatrician would monitor each child's physical health and the relationship with genetic and neurological consultants. He would consider the possibility of interventions being made in a hospital context designed for each child's particular characteristics. A social unit would take account of the help needed by families.

This centre would simultaneously fall under the headings of health, community health, research and life. This is undoubtedly an administrative heresy – but it is precisely what autistic children need.

Some years ago, we had accepted and treated a little girl with no language who presented autistic symptomatology. At the time she was leaving, I was very absorbed one day with her mother in some particular difficulties (on which we had been working for a year!) with finding a place in which she would be able to continue her treatment, which as we will see was highly promising. A small voice broke in: 'Denys, why isn't there a place?'

Echoing her question, I would ask in turn: why is this, for the moment, only a dream?

Glossary

Adhesive identification

This is the term coined by Esther Bick for the child's primary identity, contained in a psychic skin shared by the child and his mother, constituted from the holding and the immersion in language and sensations that are made possible by the mother's cathexis and her capacity for reverie (Bion). Donald Meltzer theorised a pathological version of this in autism, a clinging in a two-dimensional space in which neither the self nor the object has an interior capable of receiving projections. The sense of existence is therefore dependent on this adhesion.

Aloneness

An overwhelming need for solitude, described by Leo Kanner as an autistic characteristic, along with the need for sameness.

Autistic objects

For Frances Tustin, these are hard objects that guarantee the sense of existence through the continual sensations that they allow, or bodily sensations (muscular contractions in the tongue, muscles or sphincter) that are equivalent to those to which the child clings to avoid autistic terrors.

Autistic shapes

These are, for Frances Tustin, self-generated sensations (particularly through stereotypies) that protect the child with a self-created sensory envelope that provides a preliminary form of temporal continuity.

Black hole

Drawn from the case material of an autistic child, this is the term given by Frances Tustin to fears of annihilation, evoking the psychic *primitive agonies* described by Winnicott, which the child experiences at the separation from the breast when the absence of a representation of the internal-external boundary prevents any representation of a separation. This is then experienced as an amputation of the mouth with the nipple.

Dismantling

Introduced by Donald Meltzer, this term refers to the most primitive defence mechanism in autism: it is a passive splitting of the self according to the axes of sensoriality. Unlike psychotic disintegration, it is not accompanied by anxiety, and it is reversible.

Facilitated communication

A technique for assisting communication, developed for cerebral palsy sufferers, which is intended to alleviate the neurological motor incapacity that hinders expression by instigating a movement that the patient will then be able to direct towards things that will make it possible to understand what he wants (a picture of symbols or letters).

Introjective identification

This involves access to mourning and symbolisation and it enables the ego to identify with the object's characteristics and to make them genuinely its own in the recognition of loss.

Life drive and death drive (Freud)

In his second theory of drives, contemporaneous with the second topography (id, ego, superego), Freud – aware of something '*Beyond the Pleasure Principle*' – changed his formulation of psychic conflict. He opposes a life drive that associates the libido with the self-preservative drives (opposed in the previous model) to a death drive that seeks the end of all tension and leads towards the self-destruction of the individual himself. The external deflection of the death drive by motricity, in the form of sadism or mastery, is therefore vital for the individual. The fusion of the two drives, indispensable to life and accomplished internally by primal masochism at a primitive stage, thus becomes possible through the cathexis of the object by the two drives. This involves a libidinal and aggressive drive economy with external objects, dramatically impeded in autism. The decathexis of objects results in a defusion of drives.

Projective identification

According to Melanie Klein, this consists in the projection of a split-off part of the self *into* the object, and in its active and omnipotent control. This is a psychotic mechanism that enables badness to be expelled, and with Melanie Klein's successors and in particular Bion, this becomes a prototype for psychic exchange that can operate in the service of communication and emotional exchange.

Sameness (Kanner)

This is a very important need felt by autists for the environment to be immutable, which is a characteristic of the illness. Whereas strong appeals appear to be ignored, the child may react with a dramatic anxiety attack to minute changes in the world around him (which thus involves a degree of perception).

Stereotypies

These are repetitive self-stimulating movements that are one of the symptoms of autism. They combine movements with bodily sensory or kinaesthetic sensations that result from them: for example, flapping hands in front of the eyes, projecting saliva into the air, rhythmic swaying, knocking a part of the body or knocking a part of the body against external surfaces. They can thus become self-mutilating, especially when the child is left in his isolation without any treatment.

Symbolisation

A psychic activity *par excellence*, symbolisation involves the relationship to other people as well as the accession to an internal world. As the foundation of communication and thought, bringing the possibility of something representing something else for another person, this enables the transition to be made from the need to the drive, for example in breast-feeding, with the double displacement emphasised by Jean Laplanche, metonymic for the object – from the milk to the breast – and metaphorical for the goal – from ingestion to incorporation. It is also the symbolisation of absence in the game with the cotton reel played by Freud's grandson, as he masters first the disappearance and reappearance of the object, then his own disappearance and reappearance in the mirror.

Theory of mind

For cognitive theorists, communication involves an awareness of the mind of others as separate from one's own. According to Uta Frith, this boundary has not been acquired in infantile autism and she regards the lack of a theory of mind as an essential component of autism, which accounts for the incapacity for pretence, play or lying.

Thing-representation, word-representation (Freud)

These are metapsychological terms by which Freud distinguishes the representation of a thing, which originates from visual perceptions through the cathexis of mnemic traces that belong to the unconscious, from the representation of words, auditory in origin, which is connected with thing-representations in the preconscious-conscious.